THERE ONCE WAS A CROOKED LADY

A COLLECTION OF MEDITATIONS BY

PATRICIA FITZPATRICK

xulon
PRESS

There Once Was A Crooked Lady
A Collection Of Meditations
by Patricia Fitzpatrick

Printed in the United States of America

ISBN 978-1-60647-729-8

www.xulonpress.com

This book is dedicated to:

~ _My parents, Jim and Bettie Fitzpatrick....._

~ _My brothers and my loving family....._

~ _My most precious friends, teachers, and mentors, Eddie and Margaret McGuiggan....._

~ _All those who came into my life and touched it for the better....._

Introduction

"Crooked Woman, huh", you might say. "Sounds a bit like a mystery or a 'who-dunnit' novel". Let me say up front, this may be a mystery, and you may wonder at the end, "who would be so crazy to admit to such a jumble of ramblings". But stick with me to the last word and maybe we will find unexpected blessings.

Yes, *I* am the **crooked** woman. Let me explain...... My body has been ravaged by Rheumatoid Arthritis for some 50-plus years. (Oops! I may have just revealed my true age—a felony for the vain woman to commit!) Fingers are bits of gnarled skin and bone... feet are stubs with curled toes... legs go east and west instead of north and south... knees are knobby... hair is sparse as a result from the many years of various medications... face is moon-shaped....... Some would pull away from such a sight, such an unusually formed person. Oh, but what a loss for them. You see, inside this bent and misshapen body lives a spirit that glows... a character of unmistakable distinction. What arrogance, you might think. But wait.... this spirit I speak of is not of my doing... the character is not mine... the spirit——the character of highest integrity—it all comes from my blessed Lord Jesus Christ—it all belongs to Him, who lives *in* me and *through* me.

Being disabled, sometimes frustration comes over me when there is a work to be worked, yet physical limitations keep me from participating. Some years ago I began to write down some thoughts as a form of meditation and study. These written thoughts were shared with some friends who in turn shared with some friends. At their encouragement, I began to share my written thoughts with the women of our assembly. This program of sharing has been one way I felt useful and contributing to God's work being done. It has helped to imprint on my mind and heart that God can use His bent and imperfect vessels to accomplish His purpose here on earth.

Again, at the encouragement of two very dear friends, I take keyboard in hand to put down some thoughts... this time hopefully deeper and more insightful. I talk with God in many different ways. For me, writing is one way I pour my heart out to my Lord. The more the relationship deepens, the more ways we find to commune with Him. I guess maybe that is what Paul and the other scripture writers were trying to get across through their writings... the holy heartburn gets hotter until it consumes your life. Then, one day you realize there isn't one thing in your life that is not connected with your Lord. Cool huh!

So, I extend an invitation to you to explore the mind—and the heart of this crooked woman. Take what is useful and let the rest lie. But throughout it all, remember that this crooked woman loves her Heavenly Father more than life itself. This is my legacy I leave behind on this earth—a few pages recording some of my communing with the God I love. May any and all glory, honor and praise be to God........ And—may God bless His imperfect vessels everywhere. *Patricia*

And when he thus had spoken, he cried with a loud voice,
Lazarus, come forth....
~ John 11:43~

Meditation 1:

CALLED BACK

"Lazarus, wasn't that your name I heard being called".... "No, it couldn't have been".... "Yeah, there it is again—He is calling you"... "no—it can't be... I just got here 4 days ago... I don't want to go back"... "When the Master calls, you must obey"... "Yes, I know, and I'm going... it's just that I love it here and don't want to leave"... "Ah, but you will be back—this is your Home for eternity"...

Lazarus had been on the other side of Jordan. He had a glimpse of all that had been promised... he had been in the presence of God and His angels... four days just wasn't long enough... he wanted to spend eternity here. But for some reason his Lord was calling him back. Reluctant, yet obedient, Lazarus answered the call He went back to the other side. His friend, Jesus, was calling him, and he must go. His friend needed him for something very important to ask Lazarus to leave such a wonderful place. Lazarus left the glory of heaven, and, his body still dressed in grave clothes, he walked out from his earthly tomb....

We all have been in a place we didn't want to leave... vacation in sunny Florida... visiting grandma's house... a warm bed. But leave we must for we were being called back to work, school, and routine life... called back to get on with every-day life Our calling may not be as purpose-filled as Lazarus being called... but back we came from paradise all the same. It wasn't so much that

Lazarus was being pulled by his desires versus being obedient to his Master, Jesus. Lazarus was finally where he had longed to be. His race was finished—he had crossed the finish line and won. He was finally going to actually meet the angels who had been watching over him... he was finally going to enjoy the stories of his forefathers first-hand... he was finally going to see God face to face. And yet, he was called back to his earthly existence, back to the struggles of his earthly life. Lazarus didn't know why—just that Jesus wanted him. Obediently—willingly—lovingly, Lazarus went back.

Surely Lazarus was overjoyed at being with his sisters and friends again—and with Jesus again. But, perhaps there was a shadow of melancholy that stuck with Lazarus. After all, he had been with God and all the Heavenly host. Even if he didn't remember it all, the melancholy was there. Well, at least that's the way I felt. I had an experience not unlike Lazarus (at least it feels similar to me). Death was eminent for me. Severe respiratory arrest and cardiac failure caused the doctors to work frantically to keep the breath and blood of life going through me. While family prayed, doctors and nurses strained to bring all their knowledge and skills together to save this thread of life that was still hanging on. At one point the situation was so bleak, the head nurse from the Cardiac Cath Lab came out to console my family. This woman joined the circle and prayed along with them for God's intervention. Several hours later, in the dark of early morning, before the sun peeks over the horizon, my eyes opened to an unfamiliar scene. I strained to look around when I spotted a familiar face in the shadows. As he wiped tears from his eyes, my younger brother whispered, "You're awake..." He went to get the rest of the family from the waiting room while I lay there in that hospital room trying to pull my brain cells together to get a grip on where I was and what was going on. As the hours and days went on, the pieces fell into place. Bit by bit the story unfolded... "You are our Christmas miracle", my mom told me... "You are the Christmas miracle for the hospital", commented the specialists as they filed in to check me... "You shouldn't be here, and especially not with full mental capacity and physical functions", they told me... "We thought we were losing you", said another… Then one doctor came to me and, after checking me over, he said to me, "We physicians can do a lot, but then our knowledge and skills stop and someone higher takes over—you are an example of that very thing". I spent the next few days getting stronger and thanking all the medical staff for their excellent care.

Once home, we tried to build a new routine adjusted to my new needs. I was so happy to have this second chance at life—this second chance to make a difference for the better in the lives of my loved ones—a second chance to impress on them how much I love them. But, in the midst of all this happiness was that shadow of melancholy. Gone was the peace I had felt in those early days after the event. Something new plagued me. Was it fear—they told me this goes with having an event as big as mine. It couldn't be self-centeredness over the mountains of attention falling off… surely I couldn't be that self-absorbed. Then one day it came to me… I was feeling the melancholy because I had been to the other side! I had been to the gates of that eternal city and had seen the finish line for this race of life. I was a bit melancholy because I was called back and was here in the physical realm again with the other pilgrims plodding along life's pathways. But mostly, I was melancholy because I couldn't remember one thing I had seen, nor one word of conversation with the angels, or my Lord's face. It was all covered in blackness and I was a blank. After such an extra-ordinary experience, how could I not remember one shred of the glories of Heaven?!? And here I was once more to carry on the race to that goal I had been to. Even though I can't remember a shred of it, I have a holy homesickness for where I had been.

In my shallow perceptions, I think there was a small piece of urgency and apprehension in Lazarus once he left the grave. He was brought back for a reason…there was a purpose only he could fulfill—and he didn't want to miss it. That's what I feel—this urgency and anxiety to understand the purpose I have been called back to fulfill. Like Paul, I long to be Home. But it is needful for me to be here. Why is it needful for me to be here? Oh, dear Lord, help me to see that need and step up to fill it. I don't want this tremendous gift of a second chance—this do-over opportunity to slip through my fingers only to go back to ordinary life with all my failures. I don't want to be a disappointment to my family—to my Lord. I have had an opportunity to come into contact with people I never would have had it not been for this experience... please don't let this opportunity slip by.

Besides the physical changes in my heart, there are other changes too. I am different—I feel different. Hopefully and prayerfully, the change is for the better. I walk in boldness and courage now, telling of God's marvelous grace and love to any ear that will give a listen. I long to be a shining star in God's crown. Sappy is the best word to describe me—to describe our family nowadays. We hug more, we call more, we say "I love you" to each other more. We didn't have a traditional Christmas holiday, but we celebrate our *gifts* every day. We speak openly about how thankful we are to be together—we speak openly about the hereafter and God. We share stories of God's goodness and speak often of the importance—and power of prayer. Society demands things from us, but we now set aside time for one another. We cherish the moments that take our breath away. We now find our thrills in the laughter of the children in the family, the meal we share together, a warm hug, a note from a friend, a book that inspires us to be better—the little unimportant things in life that now have become so very important. Our family is now determined to make each day an important event—every day is a holiday to be celebrated. We are determined to enjoy every blessing each new day brings—and, at bedtime, thank God for one more day He has given. We are determined to sweat the small stuff no more, but instead stand in the glow of God's mercy and love.

Lazarus experienced death again—this time for the last time. He is in Heaven once again enjoying all the glories it holds... his race is over. Lazarus now wears the crown of Life promised to those who overcome. No grave clothes for him—he is dressed in robes of snow white and walking with his Lord Jesus for all time. One day the death angel will come for me again. And this time I will be carried away and placed in the loving arms of Jesus. I will look into His sweet face and hear Him say, "Welcome Home Child". Until then, I will quench my *homesickness* by basking in the blessing of each day here with my loved ones, and I will strive to make good use of my second chance—my do-over. I have fixed my eyes on the goal once more......

And God said, Let us make man in our image, after our likeness: and let them have dominion over the fish of the sea, and over the fowl of the air, and over the cattle, and over all the earth, and over every creeping thing that creepeth upon the earth. So God created man in His own image, in the image of God created He him;
male and female created He them.
~Genesis 1:26-27~

Meditation 2:

MADE IN GOD'S IMAGE

Made in His own image........ Think of it —you and I have been created in God's own image! Not like the giraffe, or the bear, or the lion, or the ape—or the serpent. We were made in God's own image. Let your mind rest there for a moment before reading on.............. What does that one phrase mean... What riches does that statement contain.... Let's explore that for a time.

What does it mean to look like God? Does that mean *I* look like God!!!?? Hard to imagine, huh—especially when you and I look into the mirror. 'Surely God doesn't look like this!", says the reflection back to me. So, what does being made in God's image mean? Bible scholars have long debated over this image and what it consists of. One article retrieved from the internet tells me that the image is obviously not physical, since God is not seen by the human eye —spiritual is His nature. Thus, the image has more to do with the spiritual and possibly intellectual aspects of man. It means that you and I are individuals, capable of thinking, reasoning, making choices. We are even capable of creating to some extent by using our imaginations. God created us to enjoy His presence. Man, unlike the animals, has a capacity to become God-like; to seek God and commune with Him. We see by the record in Genesis that the first man and woman enjoyed a relationship with God where all their needs were satisfied. But what does God look like???

"What is man, that thou art mindful of him? and the son of man, that thou visitest him? For thou hast made him a little lower than the angels, and hast crowned him with glory and honour. Thou madest him to have dominion over the works of thy hands; thou hast put all things under his feet..." (Psalm 8:4-6) "This passage reflects God's original plan for mankind", says another article. Humans are like God in that they are uniquely gifted intellectually (and in many other ways) so that they may relate to God and to each other as they live as stewards of the world God has given them to manage." It goes on to say that sadly, the beauty and harmony of this original created order were shattered by the rebellion of Adam and Eve, as recorded in Genesis 3. So man and woman made their choice only to find themselves alienated from God, from each other, and the world God had created for them. They began to die physically and spiritually. Woe is me — I'm getting confused here. So, does that mean the image of God in man has been distorted forever???

The tragic fact is that the image of God in man has been marred and distorted by sin and the influence of the devil. It is one of the devil's prime purposes to erase and mar the image of God in mankind. The devil has many tools to accomplish this. Another writer suggests that in Romans 1:23-27 we see that those who change the image of God into an idol become corrupted and defiled like their idol. Greed, covetousness, chasing after wealth and riches, are all called idolatry and they cause us to lose the image of God. Spiritual deception particularly mars the image of God in us because God is spirit. We can mar God's image in us when we bring discouragement to others. We do it by evil speech, by ridicule, by oppression, by crushing God's people. We mar that precious image by breaking covenants, by violence.......by wounding, exploiting and abusing people to the maximum and considering people as having no value. Yet even in this sorry state of alienation and disharmony, humans can still reflect the image of God. God calls his redeemed, covenanted people to the highest ethical standard. They are to be like Him. (At last — hope!)

As I studied further and read more, one more article told that in the New Testament the teaching of Jesus indicates the value of human beings emphasizing their being God's image-bearers. More important, Jesus himself perfectly reflects God in His life and

18

ministry as He relates sinlessly to God, people, and nature. The restored image of God in man is brought about only by God's work of re-creation... redemption. It goes on to say in Colossians 1:12-15 and Hebrews 1:1-3, the Messiah is the true image of the invisible God. It is therefore God's purpose to conform us to the image of His Son. *"For whom he did foreknow, he also did predestinate to be conformed to the image of his Son, that he might be the firstborn among many brethren."* (Romans 8:29)... And, *"as we have borne the image of the earthly, we shall also bear the image of the heavenly."* (1 Corinthians 15:49)... Re-creation comes only by the new birth. Indeed, John 3:7 states it, *"... Ye must be born again"*. This is a spiritual rebirth and enables us to be fashioned after God... start over. Jesus' work of redemption is both compared and contrasted to Adam's work of rebellion. Those who believe in Jesus are renewed in the image of God and are expected to live as renewed people. Their destiny is ultimately to be made like Jesus, to image Him perfectly as He perfectly images God. For the Christian, then, godliness in a word is Christ-likeness. There it is! There is my foundation to build upon. Start with Jesus.... Jesus Himself perfectly reflects God.

Let's study more and explore another article........ Any discussion of the image of God would be incomplete without some mention of the glorious future that awaits those who have been renewed in the image of God. God's people may experience unhindered fellowship with Him Ever since Abraham, God's people have longed for this time when life in all its facets may be lived fully to God's glory. This glorious biblical vision of a time when creatures will fully reflect the Creator's splendor ought to provide strong encouragement to Christians who presently reflect God's likeness in an imperfect yet improving manner. When one considers that the Holy Face of Jesus is the very manifestation of the Godhead, visually represented for us in the person of Christ Jesus, then a true and sincere devotion to the Holy Face of Jesus can be seen for what it should always be—both a noble goal to achieve in our humble hearts, and a vital necessity in our lives. Devotion to the Holy Face of Jesus is devotion to the Godhead Himself, the very essence of God's Divine Nature; His omnipotent power, His supreme authority and dominion over all creation. I have it now! To reflect God's image is to reflect the image of His Son—Jesus.

One last bit of research tells us that there are some practical things we can do to enhance the image of God in ourselves and others. We need to keep our eyes fixed on Jesus. Paul talks to us about this: *"But we all, with open face beholding as in a glass the glory of the Lord, are changed into the same image from glory to glory, even as by the Spirit of the Lord."* (2 Corinthians 3:18) ... As we look at Him intently, and as we continue to look, we become more like Him. We must endeavor to see the image of God in everyone...even the most depraved and hopeless person has somewhere within him that faint glimmer of God's likeness. We can enhance the image of God in others by helping them to return to God through repentance, by giving hope and encouragement. It should be our struggle to insure that the image of Christ is formed in other people —and ourselves. Paul labored as in birth pains until the image of Jesus could be fully formed in those he loved. *My little children, of whom I travail in birth again until Christ be formed in you.....* (Galatians 4:19)

What do all these facts, opinions and discussions mean to me then? Well, the one thing I am certain of is that I have a choice— reflect God's image or distort and mar the image with wickedness and evil. I can live my life and conduct myself in a manner pleasing to God or pleasing to Satan. By earnestly striving to live a life of holiness, righteousness, honor and integrity, I reflect the image of Christ (who is the visible representation of God, remember). Or, I can live seeking after all that is lurid, decadent and wicked, bringing dishonor and shame to my Creator Who breathed the breath of life into me. Those are my options........ and yours. The task isn't hard. Just live every moment pleasing to my Father. And, when I stumble and fall, He will be right beside me holding me, encouraging me on...and loving me. The deeper I get into His Word, the more I will know His character. The more I learn about Jesus, the more I will know about His Father—and mine. So here on forward, let us look upon the Face of God with all the love and affection in our whole being, and beg God to give us the grace to always love Him. And let us do so in the name of Christ Jesus. Let us pray that the image of Christ can be perfected in ourselves and in others while there is still time. All of God's work led to the creation of people, beings made in God's image. God formed us to have fellowship with Him. God focused His creative work on us so that we would focus our worship on Him. And then, one day I will look into the mirror and see not this old earthly image with all it's imperfections, but instead I will see the beauty, and gentleness, and holiness of Christ reflecting back to me. Eyes reflecting forgiveness.... face softened by love.... a countenance of peace.

Then, I will realize that the image in the mirror is me—me transformed into the likeness of God through His Beloved Son. And others will look at me and comment, "You look so much like your Father".......

*And a voice came from heaven; You are my Son,
whom I love; with you I am well pleased."
~ Mark 1:11 ~*

Meditation 3:

LEAVING A MARK

Irene Fisher Coon... Not a noteworthy name. In fact, some who once worked by her side probably don't even recall the woman's name. Ah.... but once you've met her, you wouldn't forget the woman herself. Tall in stature, and slender... graying hair in a curt bun for years until the work of it drove her to a tidy short do... long, bony fingers with red nail polish... (Oh those red nails and bony fingers!) And, in all my recollections of Mrs. Coon, there was a 3-point nurse's hat atop her head and white nurse's hose upon her legs. The woman was a credit to her profession... the visible representation of her counterpart, Florence Nightingale. Nursing was not only an occupation for Irene Coon, but her life. In the early years of the polio era, Mrs. Coon cared for the sick children brought to the hospital. Some were abandoned by their families —some for lack of better care; some for lack of interest in the child. Mrs. Coon loved and cared for them all. So much so that she made a home for these children, tended to their physical, educational, and emotional needs on a daily basis. At one point in all this, Mrs. Coon rounded up enough interest and support to establish the Crippled Children's Hospital & School in Sioux Falls, SD. Children from all over SD came there to live, to be educated in a modified environment to meet their physical needs, to receive the medical care necessary, and to be nurtured into productive young people. Mrs. Coon bore no children herself, but had hundreds of children who loved and admired her for the caregiver she was. I was one of those fortunate ones to be under the watchful eye of Mrs. Coon.

Arthritis has ravaged my body for years leaving bent and twisted limbs in its wake. It has been the reason for over 30 surgeries and corrective procedures. Time and again I have had to learn to walk all over again. I recall at each of these times walking in the parallel bars or leaning on crutches for support, I would see my mom's face at the end of the walkway encouraging me to take one more step. And, each time I would try so hard because I would want to please her... to show her that her confidence in me to do my best was not misplaced. During those early days as a small child when the pain was so severe I just wanted to lie still and never move again, my dad would gently pick me up and carry me to the bathtub where Mom would slide me into the warm water to ease my pain and loosen stiff joints. When I wanted to sob from the pain, their caring touch and loving looks would help me push back the tears and move. Each time I wanted to give in and give up, I would feel the prayers of my loving family, the prayers of concerned friends... and I would know that I just couldn't disappoint them. Mrs. Coon and my parents soon became cohorts in my cheering section. Mrs. Coon watched over me during school hours to my mother's satisfaction... and Mom & Dad picked up where Mrs. Coon left off. All would consistently encourage with "You can do it", and "Try one more time"... and they gave looks of confidence that I actually could. Because I believed them and trusted them (and they believed in me), I would try one more time, move a little farther, and swallow back the tears. At each success we all rejoiced and cheered. And the look of pleasure in their eyes and upon their faces gave me the courage and strength to keep going. How could I disappoint these people who loved me and gave so much for me.

Stop and think... think how many people have contributed to the person you are today. Think on the lives that were sacrificed to give you a better one. Listen with your heart to the sweet words of encouragement urging you on, to never settle for less than all you could be. That's what comes to my mind when I think of Mrs. Coon and the others who saw in me a potential to be better. That's what comes to mind when I recall the times my mom held my hand and whispered, "One more, honey..." My dad would gently say, "You have it in you to do it, kid"... My Bible teacher would read it with me one more time, and then, when I finally got it, would smile and say, "You had it in you all the time"... How could I ever let them down or disappoint them by not striving to live up to what they saw in me. How could I slough off all their sacrifices of time and energy to help me... all the trust and confidence they placed in me... all the love poured over me to do and be better. So, I have made it my life-long work to take all that is good and holy and Christ-like in these people and apply it in my own life, carrying on what they gave to me.

What about our Lord Jesus... does the same not hold true with Him? Jesus ignored the bite in the words spewed at him in hate by His own people, and prayed for them. Jesus looked beyond the loneliness of isolation put upon Him, and moved on with the work before Him. Jesus pushed back the pain of the whipping and scourging from His mind to focus on the purpose for Him being here on earth. It was all to please His Father. (John 5:17) That was the life, and breath, and sustenance of Jesus' life.... live to please the Father. Jesus had a confidence in His Father and in the work He was about. And, the Father had a confidence and trust in Jesus to carry out His Will. Jesus was the visible representation of God for mankind. And, now, Jesus calls us to imitate Him by striving to live out our lives in confidence... pleasing to God in Heaven —our Father...

Don't ever let the fear of being misinterpreted as "too attached", or accused of "worshiping" a kind and good person keep you from relishing the contribution he/she made to your life. Instead, hold them in highest esteem, and keep their godly characteristics alive in you... and thank them for their influence. Take what was right and true and let the rest fall to the wayside.... then pass the good stuff on. A eulogy was once spoken. It said, "this one, we can bury his body but not his spirit. We can bury his hands, but not his work. We can bury his heart, but not his love. We can bury his identity, but not his life". I'd like to think it was one of the disciples hidden away in a locked room speaking these words of comfort and encouragement about their Lord, Jesus. Perhaps, one day, someone will speak of your contribution to his/her life and thank God for bringing you along. They will see in you the visible representation of Jesus Christ, and want to imitate that, and pass it on. And, one day, the Father will say of you and me, "See this one... In his heart he never disappointed me or let me down. This is my child, in whom I am well pleased..."

So then, brethren, we are not children of the bondwoman,
but of the free. Stand fast therefore in the liberty where-
with Christ hath made us free, and be not entangled again
with the yoke of bondage.
~Galatians 4:31-5:1~

Meditation 4:

SHEPHERD ON THE HILL

Shepherd on the Hill is an old movie made in the days of happy endings and good morals. It is a tale of a village set in the back hills of the Ozarks. This village was mostly untouched by outside civilization except for a letter once or twice a year, or a rare visit from a stranger that would set the people a'buzz. It's not John Wayne that held my interest, but another character in the story. She was a woman of dark countenance. You know the type—pinched up face, dark piercing eyes, and a mouth that was always fixed in a scowl. Molly was her name. Molly had a deep-seeded hate and bitterness that surpassed any love that might have once been there... and Molly had the capability to spread her hate and bitterness to all she came in contact with, especially her own family. The village was shrouded in fear and melancholy because of Molly's influence. Molly had convinced everyone that his/her lot in life was grim, dark and hopeless... and that is the way they lived—Until the stranger came. This stranger chose to live on the hill of "dark mourning" with his sheep, taking a stand to disprove the superstitions passed on from Molly. A good deed here... a kind word there... a smile to everyone he greeted... The stranger brought a light to break through the darkness. He lifted a burden of hopelessness and replaced it with the joy of hope. The stranger brought back to the people's hearts singing and rejoicing in one another. Molly went on to live out her life in loneliness, locked away in her world of hate and fear. But she no longer had power over the people around her.

Satan is the prince of darkness and loves nothing more than to spread his sad and sorry self around. A whisper of discontent in the right ear... a hint of displeasure in the left ear... a feeling of complacency... a taste of power... a sliver of fear... a wisp of pride... a wee piece of popularity... and away we go down the road to destruction. And, of course, we don't want to go alone, so we share with anyone who is of a mind to hear. Molly used fear to hold the people captive to her dark influence. Molly worked evil in the lives there in the Ozarks... so much evil that it wrung the life out of people. She kept the people tied to her through fear. Just like a kite tied to a string, Molly would let them soar toward Heaven only so far before pulling them back to her world. Hebrews 12:15 tells us to be careful so that the root of bitterness doesn't spring up within us, therefore defiling us. Satan works the same way. Satan is so sleeked and subtle that his prey is snared and gone before even being aware of any danger. Didn't just the turn of a word entice the woman in the garden?... Wasn't it just the dreams of a boy that caused brothers to lay out a plot?... Just the sing-song of maidens turn a friend into an enemy?... Just the clink of coins in a bag bring a man to betrayal?... Just the hint of fear of losing their power bring a group of religious leaders to shout, "Crucify Him!"?... *"For our wrestling is not against flesh and blood, but against the principalities, against the powers, against the world-rulers of this darkness, against the spiritual hosts of wickedness in the heavenly places". (Hebrews 6:12)* Satan is working in and through people. Molly is alive and thriving today. The dark influence of hate and bitterness that were Molly's lives on. Molly was a willing instrument in Satan's hands to keep a village of people from living life to it's fullest and enjoying the blessings around them. That same spirit is at work this very hour. Satan, through the Mollys of this world, is chipping away at hearts, stealing away joy, peace, and contentment. The hate doesn't come out bold-faced, but in a whisper at the right time into the right ear. The bitterness doesn't all at once flood the heart, but comes in drip by drip through constant exposure to self-centeredness. The darkness doesn't just overpower, but comes subtly as the fog moving in off the sea to cover the land.

Oh, wee Christian, don't sell your blessing for pottage. Satan wants to destroy your soul. Satan will stop at nothing to separate you and me from the safe haven found in fellowship with Christ. Satan will never cease at cutting you and me from our Lord and Master. Satan, like Molly, will use any means available to him to work his deeds of wickedness—family, friends, jobs, bank accounts—whatever works to keep us from reaching our Heavenly goal. Molly kept the people in the dark through ignorance... Satan's tool. Don't stay ignorant. Study God's Word to learn of the warnings of the devil... and the marvelous blessings of God. Don't stay in the dark. Jesus is the Light... hold tight to Him. Petition the Father for wisdom and understanding in order to not only help yourself to keep right, but to help others find their way too. We have a Shepherd on the hill whom is able to keep all those sheep who want to be kept... and defeat the works of the devil. This Shepherd sheds light, dispelling the dark... He brings hope to the hopeless... confidence to the fearful... peace to the discontent... love to the hated... Our Shepherd has power so much greater than any Molly of this world... power so much greater than the demons of this dark world. And He uses that power to protect, strengthen and uplift those who call upon His Holy Name and live according to His commands. So, the next time a Molly comes shooting her tentacles of evil and wickedness toward you and me, we will not succumb to it. We will not be instruments of wickedness. We will not fill the ears of our brethren with lies, deceit, and slander. Instead, we will stand firm and declare, "Get away from me Satan! For I claim victory for righteousness' sake in Jesus' Name".......

Our Father which art in heaven,
Hallowed be thy name...
~Matthew 6:9~

Meditation 5:

LEGACY

There are so many lessons to be taken from the jumble I am about to throw your way. May you find something in these words that strikes a thought. Take it and run with it. You never know... you may have a use for it here/there again down the road.

Not so long ago there was delivered to our house a trunk and some boxes holding the final remnants of a branch of our "family tree". The boxes/trunk held letters, trinkets, articles of clothing, newspaper clippings from 60+ years ago, religious knick-knacks, and a ga-zillion photographs of people we cannot identify. As we sifted through the paraphernalia, I couldn't help but feel a touch of sadness. We were rifling through someone's life—examining private notes, laying aside bits and pieces of what were important mementoes of a vibrant life once lived. And, what did that life—those lives stand for now? Nothing but a few outdated casino coins, a few colorful letters, and a few crucifixes that used to hang on the wall overlooking the desk where the coins were counted and the letters written—hung on the wall over a bed where maybe a prayer or three were said. What did all this tell us of the lives belonging to the faces in the photos? Nothing, because we didn't know them. Going through another's keepsakes made me take stock of mine. What do I hang on to that holds meaning only to me... what will the tidbits of my life contained in a box speak to those sorting through it all once I am long gone. What do I want to be remembered for? What legacy am I leaving behind?

Prayer is a great legacy to leave. "Dad always started his day praying for me".... "Mom always prayed for me before she closed her eyes at night"... "Grandma always prayed that I would hold on and have a good heart".... I want to be remembered for my faith, my walk in faith, my prayers. "Whenever I stayed over, Auntie always prayed with me".... "She didn't come to my games, my band concerts, but I always knew she kept me in her prayers..." That's what I want to be remembered for. That's what I remember of those close and dear to me—their care, their love, their faith, their prayers.

Prayer is real. Prayer is the means by which we talk with our loving and caring Father. "Men ought always to pray..." says Jesus. [Luke 18:1] If Jesus needed to talk with His Father in prayer, then I *really* need to talk with my Father in prayer. Prayer shouldn't be a practiced set of words... words that are foreign to every day speech. "Oh God Jehovah, I cometh to thee with things thy servant asketh of thee....." No, no... Come with an honest and open heart sharing specific needs with the Father, in everyday, down-to-earth conversation. Devout Jews wouldn't even mention God's name out loud. God was too holy to utter His name—until Jesus astounded them by speaking freely of God Almighty, Father in Heaven. Notice when Jesus teaches the disciples to pray, He starts out with "Our Father...." A father loves and cares for his children, and sees to their every need. Is our Heavenly Father any different?

I love the parable of the woman who persistently petitioned the judge until he granted her request. [Luke 18] I think God wants us to be persistent with our requests. He tells us to seek Him... I don't think He meant only once, then forget it. Through persistent petitioning for what is on our hearts we let God know we are serious about what we are asking, and it is important to us. Sometimes I begin to feel I am praying in futility because there seems to be no answer, no response from God on the matter. But during those times of silence, I must look back at the history of God answering prayer at just the right time. Don't put God on a time table. Prayer loses its value when the request is set upon a time frame. There is danger in such a time of questioning God, His ability to answer me, to see to my needs, to care about me. I must trust God and wait for His response. Remember, in Ecclesiastes 3:11, the writer talks about *"He hath made every thing beautiful in His time..."* I must recognize and acknowledge my dependence on God... trust Him as the Loving and Caring Father He is, and wait in confidence and faith. Prayer at its basic and most fundamental aspect is faith in God, that He is near and He hears. *"Now faith is the substance of things hoped for, the evidence of things not seen."* [Hebrews 11:1]

Recently I learned of a man referred to as "Tramp". Tramp was an old man who lived on the streets in the rough parts of the London area back in the early 1970's. Some film-makers came across Tramp while filming some other street people in the area. The others were in the midst of a drunken hey-day, singing drinking songs while Tramp sat alone off to the side of it all, singing his own song. "Jesus' blood never failed me yet; never failed me yet; Jesus' blood never failed me yet; there's one thing I know, for He loves me so... Jesus' blood never failed me yet....." Tramp is long gone. He didn't leave a legacy of rich land, or bank accounts, or houses. He didn't leave paintings or prose. But he did leave his song behind. In the midst of poverty, the muck and mire, this man sang of his security—faith in Jesus. And, there he was content. We will never know his name, but we do know of his love for his Lord, and his undaunted faith.

That's what I want to leave behind... not boxes of photos... not boxes of letters... not boxes of trinkets nor boxes of money... I want to leave behind a legacy of faith and prayer. When they speak of me, may they speak of my love and trust in my Heavenly Father Who loved me so. When they remember me, may they see my face light with a glow when His holy name is mentioned, and remember that I always held them close in my heart and my prayers, speaking to God as a child speaks to her Father....

Finally beloved, whatever is true, whatever is honorable,
whatever is just, whatever is pure,
whatever is pleasing... think on these things.
~Philippians 4:8~

Meditation 6:

I AM DEPENDING ON YOU

At one time or another we all have had to rely on someone else for something. As children, we relied on parents to sustain us with food, shelter, love, protection. As students we relied on teachers to show us "how" and "why" and "where". In the adolescent/teen years we relied on our peers for approval and acceptance. Now in the adult stage of our lives we rely on spouses, bosses, friends, and children to find our fulfillment in life... When we stepped into the waters of baptism we made a vow before God (and witnesses) to rely on Him for our every need. But... have we.............. Let's look at some who relied on God...

In Genesis 12, Abram was called by God to leave his homeland, his father's family, his friends, everything familiar to him to go to a strange and unknown land. Obedient and trusting, Abram packed up and moved out. (Genesis 12) We find Hannah weeping and mourning over her barren state only to get up, eat and get about her business after the man of God gave her the blessing. She trusted the man of God's word... she relied on God's faithfulness. (1 Samuel 1:9-20) A wee shepherd boy called David triumphs over the giant Philistine, Goliath, armed with only five stones and a sling... and the name of God on his lips. David's trust was not in his own strength, his weapons, or his abilities. David's confidence was in God's ability to deliver him. (1 Samuel 17:34-50) Again we find David trusting in God to right all wrongs when David spares Saul's life. Saul was seeking to destroy David. And yet, when the opportunity presented itself for David to rid himself of his enemy, David left it to God to take care of. (1 Samuel 26:7-11) Jabez believed in his God, and placed all his hope in his God. "Oh, that you would bless me..." Jabez prays to God. Then he leaves it entirely up to God to decide what those blessings would be. (1 Chronicles 4:9)

Others in the Old Testament trusted in God's faithfulness and relied on Him. Elijah, thinking he was the only prophet of God left, still took a stand against the prophets of Baal and Ashtorah. He knew God would show Himself strong through Elijah. Daniel remained faithful and true to His God because he knew God was his sustainer. As was the story with the 3 boys in the fire... these young men bravely stepped up to defend their Lord God as the one and only true God because they trusted in Him. They relied on God to bring them through to receive the promises made to their forefathers. Rahab, a harlot born and raised in a world of idiolatry relied on the promise made by some foreigners in the name of their God... Moses, Joshua, Gideon, Elisha, Ezekiel, Isaiah, Jeremiah, Job, Ruth, Esther, and the list goes on....

This kind of spirit and trust was not peculiar to only those in the Old Testament. We find Peter relying on Jesus to keep him atop the water as he walked out to his Master. (Matthew 14:22-36) Stephen had a great love and trust for his Lord... so much so that as he was being stoned and killed it's reported that Stephen had the face of an angel. As those stones found their mark, Stephen relied on God to soothe his pain, to strengthen him for what was happening to his mortal body, and to see him all the way Home. (Acts 7) Notice Paul's resolve and peace in the midst of a shipwreck taking place. Paul urges those with him to keep up their courage... *"for I have faith in God that it will happen just as He told me..."* Paul had God's Word on the matter that none would be lost, and he was going to the "bank" with it. (Acts 27:13-44)

All of these people were true-life, living, breathing people... not super heroes with extraordinary powers. Just men and women with extraordinary faith and trust in Almighty God who put His finger on each one and said, "I'll have you".... God did that with each one of us too. He persistently sent someone to us, mentioning a word in just the right place to prick our hearts to see our own need for a Christ-centered life. Jesus slept in a boat during a storm—because He was tired? Tired, sure enough... but He slept in the midst of a storm because His trust wasn't in the boat's ability to withstand the storm. His trust was in the God who would bring him *through* the storm. What about us.... where is our trust....

Remember the recorded account of Jesus in the garden... He didn't take with Him all 12 of the disciples who had been with Him the last 3 years. He took only 3 men... 3 who had proven to be good and trusted friends... helpers... comrades in the cause. Peter, James and John were invited to accompany Jesus to a quiet place to meditate and pray. Jesus instructs the disciples to sit and pray while He and His three companions go on a bit farther. Jesus tells these close to Him that His soul is troubled... He is overwhelmed by what is about to take place. He is asking them to reach out to Him by their presence... to keep watch... and to pray. Pray with Him ... for Him... for the work... for mankind. When He comes back from His time of solitude Jesus finds these three friends not praying, but sleeping. At His hour of grief and despair, Jesus found Himself abandoned by those closest to Him. Relying on His friends to comfort Him, strengthen Him and partner with Him in prayer, Jesus finds Himself alone. But then... He wasn't alone, was He. Jesus' trust and reliance was not just on these men. His trust, His faith was in God the King... God the Creator... God the Father......... Lesson there for us??????? (Matthew 26:36-46, Mark 14:32-42)

It isn't uncommon to hear some voicing concerns over what seems to be an epidemic plaguing Christians. The comments run like this: "I think many women are struggling with feeling isolated and lonely... what are we going do about it...." "We need to have close gatherings more like we used to... we don't have those anymore... Barely at all..." "Intimate times were good for talking to one another and knowing what everyone was up to and what was going on so you could encourage, cry, rejoice..." "I feel isolated from the brethren—more than I ever have..." "I just say hello and then leave"..... "We need to spend more time together!!!!!"

Maybe some of our feelings of isolation come from the demands of every-day life that keep us away from classes and other church-centered activities. Vacations, illnesses, jobs also take many off doing other things, going other places. A wise person (not me) said once to just such comments as above... "And, what are *YOU* doing about it?" From where I sit I can only say... it's important for us to keep our noses in the precious Word of God... to hold tight to one another... to reach out to one another through visits, calls, cards, prayer... make a point to get out to meet with the saints at every opportunity like classes, worship services, devotions, etc. Purposely "butt" into circles of conversation long enough to say, "I am here... I care about you... I'm praying for you... I'm not going to leave until I tell you so..." Not one Christian heart would be offended by another Christian heart interrupting a conversation long enough to extend a hand of Christian love and fellowship... surely we wouldn't. Satan is alive and doing well among us. But... so is the Holy Spirit, and the Spirit of God, and the Spirit of Christ. God instructed the Psalm writer to pen these words to encourage and edify the struggling Christian heart... *"How good and pleasant it is when brothers live together in unity..."* (Psalm 133) In trust, faith... in unity with our Lord and one another, together we will stop this contagious weed of loneliness and despair from spreading, choking, destroying. We will make a difference in one another's life for goodness, purity, holiness, godliness. We will not only proclaim our trust in Almighty God, but we will demonstrate it by our conduct. Let's remind each other of the many blessings we have in each other. Let's fix our eyes not on the struggles and tribulations of this world, but look with heavenly vision to Jesus, Christ and Lord, our rock... our refuge... our creator... our sustainer... our Savior... our friend. Scripture reminds us over and over and over again that the God we serve is trustworthy. Look at: Psalm 121... *"My help comes from the Lord... The Lord watches over you..."* Psalm 116:1-14... *"I love the Lord, for He heard my cry... when I was in great need He saved me... I will fulfill my vows to the Lord..."* Psalm 91:1-11... *"He is my refuge, my fortress, my God, in whom I trust...for He will command His angels concerning you to guard you in all your ways..."* Ecclesiastes 4:9-12... *"Two are better than one... if one falls down, his friend can help him up...though one may be overpowered, two can defend themselves... a cord of three strands is not quickly broken..."*

With promises like these, as certain as the sun rises and sets... alone, deserted, or down-hearted—we will not be separated by Satan's manipulating and deceiving ways. We will put our trust and dependence in God and in His faithfulness to His people, relying on Him to guide us and watch over us. The cord of three strands is me, you, and God. We will hold on to the cord that binds us one with another as a family. That thread can be loosened... but cannot be broken........... not if we don't want it to be.

God bless us, each one, to live our lives as frogs....   F ully
R elying
O n
G od...............

Before the cock crow twice, thou shalt deny me thrice.
And when he thought thereon, he wept.
~ Mark 14:67-72~

Meditation 7:

GUILTY

There he stood... condemned of the very thing he swore he would not do. At the time his friend needed him to stand strong and remain loyal, Peter caved Why was he so weak... he fell asleep in the garden. He forgot all the teachings of loving one another and charged at that guard, whacking off an ear... would have done much more had his teacher not stopped him. But now... now, when his friend needed him most, here Peter stood among the crowd of mockers—silent. He should have shouted out "I know him", "I know him"... "He is the Teacher... the Shepherd... the Light to this world... the Messiah... the Promised One... He is our Lord"......
But he just cowered in the shadows, saying nothing. And when he was confronted about his association with this Nazarene, Peter blatantly denied it... "I don't know this man you are talking about"... how could those words of betrayal come from his lips. Jesus had told him this would happen. Jesus knew this would happen. He even said, *"...tonight, before the rooster crows twice you, yourself will disown me..."* And Peter did just that. The worst was the look—the look on Jesus face as He turned and looked straight at Peter. What was it on Jesus face—in His eyes as He looked at Peter... disappointment?... hurt?... mercy?... forgiveness?... love?... Peter wept bitterly as shame, guilt and despair washed over him...

But Peter's story doesn't end in betrayal. In mercy and love, Jesus restored Peter. Three times Jesus asked, *"do you love me"*...

and three times Peter answered, "yes, Lord"... Jesus asked three times to get a vocal conviction from Peter... three times to keep a connection and commitment... three times to remind Peter that Jesus cared for him and didn't give up on him... three times to give Peter opportunity to be cleansed of each of his denials—an opportunity to be released from the guilt and shame. From that day forward, Peter went on to be a mighty spokesman for righteousness and faithfulness—the teachings of Jesus. He proclaimed Jesus as Christ and Lord. He confronted the Jews for crucifying their Savior. With boldness and conviction, Peter warned them, pleaded with them, devoted himself to them. And when it came time that Peter should die, it is reported that Peter requested to be crucified upside down as he didn't feel worthy to be crucified in the same manner as Jesus, his Christ and Lord....

Jesus offers cleansing to everyone. There is a divine exchange when we come into a relationship with God. When we enter into a serious relationship with God—a serious, committed relationship with Him. He takes our mess and gives His righteousness. He takes our shame and guilt and gives us His forgiveness and freedom. We give Him our ashes and He gives His beauty. He gives abundance instead of poverty. He gives rest to the weary and heavy laden. He takes our despair and gives His hope. We give Him our doubts and fears, and He gives His trust and security. We give Him our loneliness, and He gives His faithfulness. David's life was turbulent, but he kept his focus on God. David gave his fears, and God gave peace to David's soul. David penned Psalm 23 from a heart that knew not only distress, but knew the peace of God. David explains the state of his relationship with God in the first line, and then he goes on to speak of all the blessings that are found in his relationship with God. "...*The Lord is my Shepherd.... He restores my soul... He guides me in paths of righteousness......*" It's a psalm of love and testimony. The man and woman in the garden have a similar story to tell. They loved God, communed with God, and He took care of them. Yet, despite all His goodness, these two turned from the One who loved them to listen to dribble from the sleeked serpent. In shame, the man and woman tried to cover their guilt and hide. But everyone knows you can't hide from God. He was disappointed with these two He had created in His holy image, but He continued to care for them. He clothed them with His mercy, His love. The same is there for us too...

David, and Peter, the harlot, the thief, a zealous persecutor of Christ's church—all have known relief from guilt and shame. All have been freed from their bondage by one and the same source— Jesus Christ, Lord and Savior. Jesus tells us that we can rise above the ashes of our broken life, but we must give up the junk—fear, anger, bitterness, guilt, etc. We must give it all up and promise not to pull it back out again to look at it from time to time. Give it all up and let Jesus fill us with His Spirit. Feel the glorious peace that comes from being washed in the redemptive blood of Jesus. Feel the deep relief that comes from being freed from guilt, shame, and failures. Bask in the warmth of a love so deep and wide and high that nothing can remove it. We, too, can look into the face of Jesus, and when He asks us "do you love me"—we can say like Peter, "Lord, you know we do"....

*"For I know the thoughts that I think toward you, saith
the LORD, thoughts of peace, and not of evil,
to give you an expected end....
~ Jeremiah 29:11 ~*

Meditation 8:

MY HERO

Let me introduce you to Jeremiah Joseph Tennessen —a.k.a.: "*Jay*". This is a young man near and dear to my heart. You see, he is my nephew. But more than being my nephew, Jay is my newest hero. Please indulge an old auntie her stories and maybe at the end you will find a new hero too.

Seventeen years old, starting his senior year in high school, a steady girlfriend, potential college scholarships in both football and basketball, a car of his own, a job that was more fun than work, a cell phone... life was good. But one day that all changed. Labor Day weekend, 2004, Jay was diagnosed with Chronic Myelogenous Leukemia (CML). The medical staff tried to be reassuring, but all Jay and his family heard was that dreaded word, "*Leukemia*". "People die from Leukemia", said Jay's dad. His mom barely left his bedside... his girlfriend cried... his brother and sister rushed to the blood bank to give blood, wanting to do something....... We all prayed. This vibrant boy with his over 6-foot body stretched out in a hospital bed looked at me as I walked up to his bedside, tears slipping away down his cheek (and mine), and asked, "Why me... what did I do to deserve this... what are we going do....." I gently and lovingly stroked his brow, speaking soft and low, "We are going to trust God"........

In the hours and days that followed, I searched my mind to find answers to questions coming at me from Jay, his family, and my own.

This boy was hardly ever sick. He was tough and healthy. Being the youngest of three in the family, he fought hard to not be left behind. And, being the youngest he quite often played the role of guinea pig or scapegoat. Scanning the years I recalled his having chicken pox right along with his brother and sister... the time he called 9-1-1 to ask if they knew where his great-grandma was... the afternoon he tried his great-grandpa's smoking pipe... the way he flew down our ramp on his big wheel.... Jay had always been a good boy... a loving, robust, healthy boy. However did he come up with leukemia?!?!?!!? Why was God allowing this horrible thing to happen to this young man with so much life to live yet??? Then the answer came as gently and softly as a summer breeze—and as definite and certain as night turning to day. The issue isn't so much God allowing bad things to happen—but instead, it's that God is true to His promise. *"...for he hath said, I will never leave thee, nor forsake thee..."* (Hebrews 13:5b) He will never leave us, nor forsake us. God is right beside Jay blessing him and tending to his every need. I took this revelation and passed it on to Jay. "You have been blessed with leukemia, Jay, to be a blessing to others....... God chose you out of all the millions of senior kids and knew you could do this—bless others through your ordeal...." And, bless them he has...............

Sometimes we Christians tend to get puffed up a bit with our own holiness. We sometimes (unintentionally I believe) look down our righteous noses upon others who are not "like us" and say a poo-poo on anything not of our thinking or doing. Well, let me tell you——I have been brought to my proverbial knees by the events of Jay's trek with leukemia. Jay and his family have been overwhelmed with the goodness of people around them. The word spread. Through treatment and determination Jay was well enough to play basketball. At each game the word spread of this amazing senior who was fighting to overcome his disease. The television and newspaper people took hold of Jay's story and spread it even farther. Boys' State Basketball Tournament came and Jay got the release from his doctor to go with the team. My hero played his heart out (even after getting a broken nose!) and his team won 4th place.... and the word spread. There was no harshness, nor bitterness at the tournament—only friendly competition and everyone cheering on a boy fighting for his team—

and his life. Someone at the grocery store... the one sitting in the next chair at a school program... the pharmacy's delivery man.... the receptionist at the dentist's office... they all have heard Jay's story. Jay has touched lives with his determination and positive attitude—his strength and courage. He is blessing others through his blessing.

Through the many foundations associated with leukemia, Jay was provided with his own web site. People could visit the site, catch up on Jay's progress, and leave messages for Jay and his family. There had been over 30,000 hits from early March, 2005 to September, 2005. My own visits are limited to reading only 2 or 3 messages and then I need to stop—my eyes begin to "*sweat*". The outpouring of care and concern is amazing. The thoughts and prayers envelope the family and buffer the bad days. People who didn't know Jay but heard of his story were leaving messages of encouragement. "You are in our thoughts and prayers....... We pray for you daily...... Our class prays for you each morning.... Look to God for your strength.... You are a great inspiration to me.... Trust God.... Remember Philippians 4:13.... "The messages were consistent from young and old, male and female. Never before outside of a church setting have I heard so many talk so openly about their faith in God. Never before have I witnessed such an outflow of kindness and caring. Why is it we hear so much focused on the bad things people do and not a twitter about all the good?

Jay is my hero because he brought me back to the place I began so long ago—loving God and loving people. Through Jay I am reminded that God is always with us, especially through the bad times. Through Jay I see good in the world again. Are all these well-wishing, praying people blood-bought Christians? I haven't a clue. But, I do know the genuine prayer of *anyone* is quick to be heard by our Loving Father. And I believe these people who took the time to write on Jay's web site had a genuine care and concern for this boy and his family. I truly believe their prayers were heard. It would be a sad and sorry thing to dismiss all the good being done because these are not *saved souls* as we know it to be according to God's Word. God uses every vessel to accomplish his work.... a harlot, a Babylonian king, a fisherman, a tax collector......... a sinner like me. I pray for these that they have deepened their awareness of God as they have blessed our family. I have been touched by the encouragement that was sent to Jay. I have been humbled by how quickly so many reach in and give, whether it be from their pocketbooks or their hearts. I see in these people the clear picture of the parable of the Good Samaritan. I see how simple it is to tell a story and see it spread. I see how hungry the world is for inspiration and a godly hero to look up to. I see I am not alone in my prayers. I see in Jay the clear picture of what I need more in my life—willingly and joyfully accepting God's Will for my life, and Trusting God. God has used Jay to bring a mass of people together in a common cause—the well being of another. Our beloved Jay died on September 9, 2005. But, the kind and thoughtful deeds and encouraging words keep coming—and the prayers keep going up. Our entire family stands with tear-filled eyes saying a prayer of thanksgiving for the multitudes who have shown us that God is alive in the hearts of so many............ and all glory, honor, and praise to God for giving us our hero, Jeremiah Joseph Tennessen......... *Jay.*

"Then again called they the man that was blind, and said unto him, "Give God the praise: we know that this man is a sinner". He answered and said, "Whether he be a sinner or no, I know not: one thing I know, that, whereas I was blind, now I see"
~John 9:24-25~

Meditation 9:

I DON'T KNOW...

Oone day some men were sitting at the gate doing their usual afternoon visiting, they noticed an unusual amount of commotion going on this afternoon with people scurrying here and there. A sense of excitement was in the air. "What's going on?", one said to another... "Is there a nobleman riding through the town?", said another... "Wait a minute—isn't that the lame man... look he is running!", commented one of the men. To this replied a deaf/mute who just passed their way, "Yes, it is".... In astonishment, the men gathered around this one who was once unable to speak... "Tell us more... how did this miracle happen... how did *all* these miracles happen?"... The deaf/mute spoke as he was leaving, "I haven't the time to explain to you... I'm off to do mission work and spread the good news... go ask the blind man—he saw it all".....

Here this man is... blind since birth. And now, because he came across this Nazarene, the one called Jesus, he can see—see the color of the sky... see the birds in flight... see the sparkle of sunlight on the water... see his parents faces... Instead of rejoicing with him, the Pharisees want to interrogate him... "How did this happen", they shoot at the man. He tried to explain about the spittle on the ground, the mud, the washing in Siloam's pool. But the Pharisees wouldn't listen. Finally, in frustration, the man said, "I don't know... one thing I *do* know is once I was blind, but now I see"... "*I don't know*"— a hard statement for a person to admit. This man didn't know the details of what caused the spittle mixed with dirt, the water from the pool to heal him. He didn't know how it all worked together to heal eyes that had never seen. But he did have a story to tell, and he stuck to it. Facts plain and simple... *"Whereas I was blind, now I see."* (John 9:25)

Don't you just admire those people who can recite scripture word for word... and especially those who can hear a phrase and snap off exactly where to find it in the Bible. And, don't you sit in awe as a person can just rattle off, "oh, that scripture means——"...

It's a great talent and gift. I have benefited from such people and tried to imitate them. Ask a biblical question, and they have the answer. For me, however, I am still picking up only the gem lying on the surface. You would think that after so many years as a Christian and Bible student, I would be able to recite something, or expand on the book of Isaiah or Revelation! But no—here I am still skimming the surface. Makes me feel less than where I should be in my Christian walk... less than what —and who I should be.

On the other hand, I do know some things for certain. I know that Jesus is the son of a Jewish virgin named Mary. I know that Jesus is the Son of God. I know that Jesus died on the cross as a sacrifice one time for all time to atone for my sins. I know that Jesus is my Salvation. I know that God has a plan and a purpose for my life. I know that God can use ordinary people to work His extra-ordinary work. I know that Jesus works miracles still today. I know that the more I know Jesus, the more I love Him. And the more I love Jesus, the more I want to know Him.

Isn't it amazing (and a bit silly) that even as an adult the one big truth in my life comes from a child's song —*"Jesus loves me, this I know, for the Bible tells me so"*.... "Why is it that adults find it so hard to say "I don't know"? Grown-ups have a talent for making things so complicated. I have come to the conclusion that the simple, straightforward answers are the best. I may not be able to quote scripture verbatim, but I do know that the blood of the Lamb of God washes me clean over and over again. I know that scripture tells me that the blood will cover my sinful nature and make me a new creation. I know that reading scripture keeps me going even though the way may be hard. I know in my heart that God will not bring on me anything that I am not able to get through. He will walk beside me—or carry me through. I know that in scripture I find comfort when loneliness looms close. I know without a doubt that God promises He will never leave me nor forsake me. Because I love my Heavenly Father, I hunger to know more about Him... and the way to do that is to look at His Son, Jesus... and the way to look at Jesus is to get into the Book... His Book... the Bible.

One day as I sat in my ignorance and feeling sad, a thought— a plea came to my heart—and then a song—"tell me the story of Jesus... write on my heart every word... tell me the story most precious... the sweetest that ever was heard..." Then the light bulb snapped on! I don't need to be able to explain in intricate detail how I know Jesus is my Friend... I just need to tell of the glorious things God has done in my life—and is still doing! The facts are I came to God broken and in despair. He pointed me to the cross and said, "I love you that much". Jesus knocked at my heart's door, and I let Him in. He replaced despair with hope. He took my brokenness and made me whole again. He took my sagging soul and filled it with the Holy Spirit. I do remember stories in the Bible of people who, when God put His finger upon them, they were able to rise above their circumstances and do glorious things for God, fulfilling His purpose. It is important to read and study the Bible in order to get a clear picture of God and His tremendous love for man. It is vital to the wellbeing of the soul to spend time in God's word. It restores, revitalizes, and energizes. Each time we open up the Good Book something new and wonderful leaps from the page—even if the page has been read a hundred times before. New insights await on the pages. Encouragement to continue on is spoken in the words of the scriptures. Freedom from a guilt-ridden heart is found in the words of our Lord. Redemption is there when we need it. A plan for living life abundantly is there. Our heritage is recorded in this precious Book. Images of our Father are on the written page. I just need to go and tell what I do know—what is written on my heart...

I am not a scholar. I can't explain how the stars stay in the sky, or where the wind comes from, or how daffodils know when to pop up and bloom. I can't exegete the book of Deuteronomy, nor can I explain every particle in Solomon's building of the temple, or can I even quote scripture all that well. But, I do know in Whom I believe...who it is that picks me up time and again and sets me back on the path that leads Home. He saw me in my brokenness and loved me and called me to Him. I say in honesty and humility, I don't know a lot of things—but I know where to go for an answer. I know where to go to get help for any situation I might be in—more importantly, I know *Who* to go to for my help. One thing I know for certain—I once was blind, but now I see. I see with heavenly vision and long to be with my Father and to look into the eyes of my Lord, Jesus—the One Who gave it all for me. So—if you want an explanation regarding the deep meaning of Jesus, His miracles, and things in the Holy Bible, go ask the blind man—he saw it all..............

He shall cover thee with his feathers, and under his wings
shalt thou trust: his truth shall be thy shield and buckler.
Thou shalt not be afraid for the terror by night;
nor for the arrow that flieth by day…
For he shall give his angels charge over thee,
to keep thee in all thy ways…
~Psalm 91:4-5, 11~

Meditation 10:

AFRAID OF THE DARK

Remember when you were a young child and the dark was a frightening thing to you…. You would ask mom to leave a light on, your favorite stuffed animal was tucked under your arm to guard you through the night, and the blanket was securely pulled up so far that only your eyes were left uncovered. The years passed and we grew older, we laughed at the dark, told scary stories in the dark. Yet with all our bravery we still ran for that safe place the moment a noise creaked somewhere out there. Even now, the dark sometimes looms over us bringing some apprehension and uneasy moments. The dark causes otherwise clear vision to be distorted and fuzzy. But it is not just the dark night that brings on these child-like feelings of distress. Darkness comes in all forms. Life brings on circumstances that cause knees to shake and nerves to rattle. While others are walking in the bright sunshine, one soul is draped in dark emotions—"what will I do if my job goes away?..... what if my paycheck isn't big enough to pay that bill?... what will I do if the biopsy shows cancer?.... how can I go on without my loved one beside me?.... how can I get that child to turn around?.... is my child safe at school and with friends?.... am I safe to go out alone?... what if I must go through life without a mate?..." The dark carries all sorts of threats—each so different, so specific and so worrisome. Darkness surrounds us and drives out the light of security, hope, and peace...

Did you know Crayola makes "glow-in the-dark" crayons?!!?!?!!?! Some years ago I did a Bible lesson for a class of first/second-graders. We talked about Jesus being the Light to the world. We talked about how we must look hard sometimes past all of Satan's junk to see the Light of Jesus. But that Light is always there if only we look, and that Light will lead us down the path set for us by our loving Lord. We placed the crayons strategically around the room, and then turned the lights out. At first the children were a bit skittish. It was really black in that windowless room! But then there was a squeal, and then another. Little bits of glow-in the-dark crayon started popping into our vision like wee bits of rainbow. The children saw a path of rainbow flickers and safely followed it around the room, not once bumping into anything or stumbling. We all left the classroom that day with a bit more understanding of the Light—of our dependence on Jesus.....

Over the last lot of years life has thrown some terrific stones at this soul. There have been more dark days than I care to admit. Yet these dark days brought me renewed understanding of how much I depend on my God. How can I explain to a young girl why her grandpa was taken away just as she was getting re-acquainted with him? I could explain to her that we thank God for bringing her back to her grandpa for a few weeks to build memories that would warm her heart. How could I comfort a friend as cancer was taking her away from her husband and children? I could tell her about a God who would work blessings for her and her family if only they would believe. How could I tell a boy with so much of his life still ahead of him that leukemia wasn't the end? I could speak with him about life everlasting, no matter what our earthly bodies went through...

God brought a song my way a few weeks back from a Gaither Homecoming series. It spoke of just this thing— —darkness—and the dark-chaser to beat all. Read a few lines from the song........*"When I'm alone and light slowly fades... cold with the night closing in...."* Did these words ever strike a nerve! Ever lie in the dark and feel the night closing in? And yet, we are so silly... instead of calling out to our Protector, we let Satan's demons push us farther under the covers. *"I know the shadow of almighty wings... Lord won't you send them again... Lord won't you send your angels to watch over me ... I'm so afraid of the dark... Lord send your angels to watch over me... wrap me in sheltering arms .... Shield me... keep me... hold me safe in your arms... Lord, send your angels to watch over me.... Wrap me in sheltering arms..."* [*He Sends His Angles*, by Suzanne Jennings/William Gaither] Notice the writer directs us to God for our safekeeping. He stands with arms open wide, inviting us to run to Him for our security...

A book I once read to a class of second/third grade Bible class students told the story of a boy who lived in a village of beauty and peace, a village surrounded by a wall. The keeper of the wall warned the children that danger awaited them should they leave the safety of the village. Well, the boy was too brave—and too curious to let any old warning keep him from scaling the wall and exploring the world beyond. It wasn't long before the boy regretted his foolish decision. The world outside was dark, cold, lonely, and full of frightening things. The boy tried to find a way back over the wall, but there wasn't any. Despite all his gallant efforts, he was stuck right where his defiant willfulness had taken him—on his own in the dark. As the boy sat in a huddled lump of tears, his heart softly cried to the Master of the village—the Keeper of the wall. "Please find me and bring me home", cried the boy. As the sobs grew stronger, the boy could feel a warmth, a change. There standing before him was the Master Gatekeeper—arms open wide in love, offering security, and ready to accept the disobedient boy and take him home. *"Sometimes the child inside of me cries... the fears of the dangers unseen.... Questions with answers I can't seem to find.... then you send your angels to me... Lord, send your angels to watch over me... I'm so afraid of the dark... Lord send your angels to watch over me.... Wrap me in sheltering arms... wrap me in sheltering arms..."* [*He Sends His Angels* continued]

Remember the servant with Elisha. He only saw the host of horses and chariots "Oh, what shall we do?," the servant asked. But Elisha saw God's hand. With a simple prayer from Elisha, the servant's darkness was replaced with hope and confidence in God's deliverance. Elisha didn't let the dark situation push away his Light of hope and confidence. God was with Elisha and his servant, and that day God delivered them from their enemy. God delivered them from the dark...

And what about Paul and Silas. It was the middle of night... sitting in a prison... a dark and hopeless place to be, one might think. But instead of sitting in despair, crying over their inability to change their circumstance, Paul and Silas were singing and praying. Singing and praying so much that the other prisoners were listening—and so was God. God heard their prayers, their praises. He delivered Paul and Silas from that darkness. In fact, God delivered Paul and Silas in such a magnificent way that the jailer became a believer through this...

The Psalm writer knew about darkness. He wrote: *"Oh, that men would praise the LORD for his goodness, and for His wonderful works to the children of men! For He satisfieth the longing soul, and filleth the hungry soul with goodness. Such as sit in darkness and in the shadow of death, being bound in affliction and iron.......Then they cried unto the LORD in their trouble, and He saved them out of their distresses. He brought them out of darkness and the shadow of death, and brake their bands"....* (Psalm 107:8-15) God dispels the darkness for the soul who calls upon His name. The priest, Zechariah, spoke of God's tender mercy and bringing a Light to shine on those living in the darkness. He would set their feet on the path of peace... that promise is for us too. The big dipper of promises comes from Jesus Himself. *"Then spake Jesus again unto them, saying, I am the light of the world: he that followeth me shall not walk in darkness, but shall have the light of life."*..... (John 8:12) And there you have it... the eternal Light bulb for a dark world...

The lesson here is not so much to remember scripture verses, nor the words to a song—but remember the theme to these. Darkness comes into our lives—if not yet, wait for it will come. But the darkness doesn't last but only for the night—then morning comes. God is our mighty refuge, our hope, and our perfect peace. Lean on Him. Call to Him. Let God be your "night-light". Instead of seeing only the dark of night, let God open your eyes to the stars lighting the night. Let God wrap you in His sheltering arms..........

For I am persuaded, that neither death, nor life,
nor angels, nor principalities, nor powers,
nor things present, nor things to come,
Nor height, nor depth, nor any other creature,
shall be able to separate us from the love of God,
which is in Christ Jesus our Lord.
~Romans 8:38-39~

Meditation 11:

WHAT'S IN A NAME

Mephibosheth….. who would name his/her precious baby "Mephibosheth"?!!?!?!!? It's not a name that just rolls off the lips and makes a pleasant feeling come over a person. Can you imagine being a child and trying to learn to spell a name like Mephibosheth?!!? Sure wouldn't find a key chain or a book bag or a trinket with that name written on it. Then, again, it is a name one wouldn't soon forget. Nor is it considered a common name like Bob, Joe, John, or Bill. Apparently in the days of King Saul the name, Mephibosheth, was a name of distinction because Jonathan, son of Saul, gave it to his son. Although the boy was heir to the throne which ruled over Israel, he never was given the opportunity. In fact, Mephibosheth really didn't grow to be a giant-slayer, or a ruler of kingdoms, or a mighty warrior. But his life was of significance to some degree because he is mentioned in at least two pieces of scripture…

Mephibosheth was five years old when his father and grandfather were killed at the hands of their enemies. In fear for the boy's life, his nurse picked up Mephibosheth and fled for safety. But as the nurse hurried to leave, Mephibosheth fell and became crippled. Life for a cripple in old Israel was a life of constant hardship. For years Mephibosheth lived dependent upon the kindnesses of others. Then one day a messenger summoned Mephibosheth to come stand before King David. In the king's presence, Mephibosheth bowed down to pay honor. "Mephibosheth", said David…. "Your servant", Mephibosheth replies…. "Don't be afraid", David said to him, "for I will surely show you kindness for the sake of your father Jonathan. I will restore to you all the land that belonged to your grandfather Saul,… and you will always eat at my table"… Mephibosheth bowed down again and said, "What is you servant that you should notice a dead dog like me"… David summoned his servant and commanded, "Mephibosheth shall always eat at the king's table"…. And that he did…. A nice story with a happy ending. But look closer. There is a wealth of lessons to be learned from Mephibosheth's story. This boy with a strange sounding name can help us to live a rich life—the life of an heir to the Kingdom, always to sit at the King's table…

First, there is the covenant between David and Jonathan. "Do not ever cut off your kindness from my family", was the oath Jonathan and David made to each other. It was a covenant of friendship and love … an oath made with God as witness. We have that same promise —covenant—from our Lord. He promised to never leave us, nor forsake us. God promised Abram that He would be Abram's shield and great reward. He promised Abraham and Sarah a child in their old age, and Abraham would be the father of nations. God promised David that his seed would always be on the Throne. God promised a remnant would always remain in Israel. God promised Moses a deliverance. Joshua told the Israelites to remember that not one of all the good promises God made to them had failed. He promised we would be heirs to His Kingdom if only we remain steadfast in our faith, and ours is the crown of Life. God promised that none should perish if only they believe. God promised a Comforter, Counselor, Peacemaker, Way to Life Eternal, a Savior… Promises / covenants made….. Promises / covenants kept…

Next, we see Mephibosheth bowing in the presence of King David. Mephibosheth did this as a token of respect and honor, recognizing David's position. Mephibosheth, a lowly crippled boy, fatherless and homeless, came in humility and recognized, respected, and honored the king. He recognized David as king—he acknowledged David as king… and he recognized David's power—power to bless or to curse. Can we say the same for ourselves? Do we recognize and acknowledge Jesus as our King? Do we recognize and acknowledge God's power to bless and to curse? This is an area where the Pharisees struggled. They could not—would not see Jesus as the King finally come as prophesied from old. They would not, could not see—but the blind man did—the lame did, the sick and downtrodden did... the hopeless did. So did a bunch of fisherman, a tax collector, a lady of ill-repute, a short little man, a royal official, a thief on a cross, the lame, demon-possessed, blind, sick, Jew, Gentile, poor in spirit.... Even creation itself bows to its Creator, Lord and King. The soldiers thought they were mocking Jesus when they placed that sign on His cross. Little did they know they were proclaiming what so many already knew——*"Jesus of Nazareth, King of the Jews"*....

Comfort..... Notice that David offers comfort, compassion, and reassurance to Mephibosheth. This son of Jonathan has known only the life of the fatherless. And, now, here he is called before the king. Uneasy and uncertain, the boy bows as a servant before his king. He has been living in a house belonging to another, in a town little known to anyone. Now Mephibosheth is in the king's house, in the king's presence. What is to become of him? David immediately sets the record straight—no playing games... no guessing... "Don't be afraid", David tells Mephibosheth. And then, David lays out his plan.... a plan to offer Mephibosheth a life more fitting for a descendent of a former king. A plan to uphold his end of the oath with his beloved friend, Jonathan. David knew fear... and David knew the warm feeling of being reassured. God had long been David's strength and refuge. Now David was offering that to the son of his friend. Jesus offers comfort. He tells His disciples, "Don't be afraid of a storm, don't be afraid of what you are seeing, don't be afraid of my leaving you, don't be afraid of the world"....

Jesus tells a distraught father "Don't be afraid... just believe and your child lives". Over and over again Jesus reassures and comforts His followers. Throughout the Bible are reminders of where our comfort and security lies. Throughout the scriptures is the plan for God's people to sit at the King's table forever—a plan to live as a child of the King... a plan to live forever in the presence of our Loving Father. Comfort—compassion—reassurance to rely on? "Be strong and courageous. Do not be terrified; do not be discouraged, for the Lord your God will be with you wherever you go"...... God said it... Then it is so... Comfort to rely on....

Mephibosheth found blessings in his meeting with the king. He considered himself unworthy to receive grace from the king... "What is your servant that you should notice a dead dog like me", said Mephibosheth. He didn't make demands, he did not go away to plot out how to get back what was his due. After all—wasn't he the grandson of King Saul... Mephibosheth knew only that this man whose presence he was in now was showing great mercy and kindness to him. And he felt unworthy of such a great gift. After all, he had done nothing to earn it—he was just a dead dog. We can also find blessings each time we meet with our King. Matthew 5 speaks of those who would be blessed... "Blessed are the poor in spirit..., those who mourn..., the meek..., the peacemakers..., the pure in heart...", and on the list goes. Scripture instructs us on how to receive these blessings. We must seek God first...... Seek God first... The blessings come from God. We must go to the Giver of Blessings... humble ourselves in His holy presence for we, too, are just like dead dogs doing nothing to earn the rich mercy and grace of a loving King. In Him is rest for the weary soul, cleansing for the spirit. Through Him we can drink at the well and never thirst again. Through God's gift we can enter the Kingdom of God. Because of the Gift, we are freed from our sins by His blood, and made a kingdom and priests to serve God forever. Before us stands the blessing to share in the glory of Jesus Christ. In Romans we are promised the blessing of becoming co-heirs with Jesus. The blessings are laid out for us plain and simple. Don't need a shovel to dig them up. Here we are, lowly and looking into the face of God. We ask, "What is your servant that you should notice a dead dog like me"... God smiles and replies, "Because I love you"... And the scripture writers proclaim it in John 3:16..."*God so loved the world (that's you and me), that He gave His one and only Son, that whoever believes in Him shall not perish, but have eternal life*".... Blessings.... AMEN!

What's in a name? Mephibosheth —an uncommon name. An unforgettable name. A name that, when spoken, should bring to mind a host of precious jewels —gems of scripture rich with lessons for us. Mephibosheth—holds within the sound of it covenants, oaths, and promises. It shines with humility, respect and honor for the King. It warms us with thoughts of comfort and reassurance. And it should cause to spring within us an appreciation for blessings .... a *wealth* of blessings if we but only pick them up. Mephibosheth—a name I'll not soon forget............

...for the LORD seeth not as man seeth;
for man looketh on the outward appearance,
but the LORD looketh on the heart.
~1 Samuel 16:7~

WORTHLESS

The afternoon sun was warm as it streamed through the window. It seemed a stark contrast to the frigid winter temperature outside. Pitter-Patt settled her old body back into her favorite chair to rest aching bones from the day's chores. As her body rested, the woman's mind wandered... "Another birthday coming up.... What has it all been about?.. What am I leaving behind when I go?... What has my life amounted to?... I have no husband, nor children to leave a mark on... Have I made any difference for anyone? I am just a worthless life." Melancholy fell over the woman...

A child's face popped into the woman's mind-~tall, lanky, tattered around the edges, nobody liked this child. She was left out of playground games, left out of birthday parties, left to her own. Even her name was nothing special—Claudell. And thus, the child acted up to get attention—any kind of attention was better than none. There was a second child—Pitter-Patt was small, pudgy, and crippled. This second child was also left out of the playground games, parties, etc, because of a frail physical stature. Pitter-Pat sat alone in the classroom during recesses and gym classes. One day while Claudell was sentenced to spending recess inside as punishment for her bad behavior in the classroom, the two children struck up a conversation over the book the crippled child was reading. Recognizing common ground of loneliness in the two children, the teacher paired the tattered girl with the little crippled girl. They spent a week together during recess, one reading and the other learning to read better. More importantly, these two girls giggled and shared what all children long for—belonging. Accelerating health problems caused Pitter-Patt to spend the rest of the school year at home. However, when planning her birthday party in the spring, the crippled girl insisted that the first on her list of guests was her lanky friend, Claudell. A smile crossed the old woman's face as she remembered the gift Claudell brought to the party—a box with baby chicks inside peeping their little selves silly...

As quickly as this vision had come, it was replaced with another—this one of a teen-aged neighbor girl. Pitter-Patt and Ethelyn had been playmates for most of their childhood, spending hours playing with paper dolls and barbies. Now the teen was scarcely seen. She stayed to her own house and school. Then one day the teen's secret was obvious —Ethelyn was having a baby. Pitter-Patt gathered her allowance to offer a baby gift to her friend. Such a look of embarrassment, shame—and relief fell on Ethelyn's face as tears rolled down—and a friendship was restored. Not so many years later Pitter-Patt's heart ached at the loss of Ethelyn from a terrible accident. Instead of going to the funeral, Pitter-Patt sat next to the hospital bed of Ethelyn's daughter, reassuring the child that everything would be ok in spite of her mom being taken away...

Again this vision was gone, and another came. This new vision was of a young woman struck with muscular dystrophy and bound to a wheelchair and a breathing apparatus. The girl had a lonely existence in a desolate part of the state, living with a bitter mother and siblings who were embarrassed by their sister's needs. The two crippled girls, Pitter-Patt and Lollie-June, had become fast friends during their time at a special school. Now they were going to spend a brief time together at Pitter-Patt's home. However, the brief time turned into three months. The girls listened to music, played games, went shopping, went to movies, enjoyed Pitter-Patt's family, and shared secrets in the dark of the bedroom they shared. Lollie-June asked repeatedly to be adopted by Pitter-Patt's family, and everyone laughed. Not until some months later when the letters were desperate, did they realize this friend was serious. Lollie-June died alone in a hospital with only the kindness of nurses and memories of a friend's love to comfort her...

As this picture brought tears to Pitter-Patt's face, another vision popped into her mind's eye—dark eyes flashing and a big smile. "Oh, how pleasant!", thought the woman. It was her co-hort from work. Pitter-Patt and Myra had spent 20-plus years working side by side. But more than that, they shared a deep friendship over the years. Pitter-Patt was there when Myra's wedding was announced. She was there when Myra's babies were on the way. She was there to look up and share a giggle at Myra's face, her eyeglasses on upside down because the work day was just too long. Pitter-Patt was there filling in for "mom" because she was away from her desk for a moment when someone needed to take phone calls for Myra from home to settle a sibling squabble, or listen to Myra's little boy give the weather report for some far-off place from the weather channel. Pitter-Patt was there when the crazy teen years drove Myra to the brink and homework for a boy was near impossible. Pitter-Patt was there when Myra discovered a lump. She was there to rejoice with Myra because chemo treatments were completed. She was there to fetch a damp cloth for a fevered brow when this strong-willed Myra sat at her desk, trying to work and keep life normal as cancer was ravaging her. Pitter-Patt was there to stroke that brow and whisper words of faith as cancer was winning the battle. She was there to offer hugs of comfort and support to Myra's hurting husband and family as they all said good-by to their precious loved one...

Again tears rolled from the woman's closed eyes. So lonely again. No one to confide in, to share secret fears and hopes with. As darkness was about to enfold the woman, she was reminded of faces so loving, so caring, so genuine. One face was of an elderly Christian brother who was always ready with a big bear hug. His low baritone voice could be heard above all the others, especially during singing. When age and illness forced this kind man to remain home-bound, Pitter-Patt sent cards, sent e-mails, made visits, and even made a tape of her own voice singing for her friend to play and sing along. Though the quality was minimal, the effect was max. On so many visits, this gentle soul would say to Pitter-Patt, "I don't know why I am still here—God must have one more thing for me to do..."

Pitter-Patt would counter with, "God knows we aren't ready to let go yet"... Once we were, this soul was lifted heavenward... And this woman was there to bid another precious friend farewell...

As Pitter-Pat sat fondly on this memory, two more faces came to mind. These were the faces of her "alien" friends. How precious this vision was. These people came just at the right time. They brought a new understanding of faithfulness and holiness—a new understanding of our greater purpose in life. They brought true and lasting friendship, seeking only Pitter-Patt's greatest good. As she basked in this pleasant vision, it was pushed over by the reminder that these precious friends had moved on to continue the work God had placed before them—this time in another country, back to their homeland. How could it be? They came and then were taken away so quickly. And just when Pitter-Patt would need them most. Pictures upon pictures—visions upon visions—faces, events—it all came like a parade across Pitter-Patt's mind. some made the woman smile—children's wee tokens of love, a devoted dog by her side, a mother's touch... Some made the woman tearful—the passing of a beloved and dear father, uncles, grandparents, friends. Some even made the woman chuckle in her sleeping state—silly times with brothers, nephews, nieces, cherished friends.

Then a boy's face popped into view like a shooting star... bright blue, sparkling eyes that spoke of his zeal for life... first the boy was riding his big-wheel... then he was tying night crawlers together... next he was eating the biggest bowl of ice cream... next he was shooting baskets. He was always ready with a smile and a hug. "Oh no", groaned the woman as she saw the boy lying in a hospital bed so sick. She had told JJ at the onset of his illness to trust God. Now she needed to tell herself. She couldn't explain to JJ's mom why her youngest child was the one chosen to bear this. She couldn't explain it to herself. She could only be there for the mom, for the dad, for the boy, for the family, and be a link to the "Anchor" through this storm. On the occasions when visiting JJ, Pitter-Patt would offer soft words of faith and love to the boy in spite of his coma. She would hold his hand, caress his arm, stroke his brow, speak softly words of everlasting hope. When death was imminent, Pitter-Patt stood at the boy's bedside along with his family, and held his mother's sobbing face to her breast as the family let him go...

A flood of memories came over Pitter-Patt. There was a loving father who was taken abruptly from the family. He had worked hard all his life taking care of the needs of his family, both financially and emotionally. And mom—she was there too, always giving of herself. Even now, Pitter-Patt smiled at how mom still gave and took care of family while others her age were resting on their laurels and their kids. There were the grandparents who were doting on Pitter-Patt in her childhood... the children who accepted the crippled girl as an equal... the friends who accepted the crippled woman as an equal... the older Christian brother who was always ready with a hug and a word of encouragement for a sagging heart... the special aunts and uncles who tried to take away the pain by offering their presence during all those hard times... two brothers who gave love in place of jealousy because their crippled sister's condition demanded so much of their parents' attention... a mother and father who gave up so much of their lives for the crippled child... children who came for Bible class and accepted this crooked and bent woman as their teacher... parents who entrusted Pitter-Patt with their children's spiritual teaching... doctors, nurses, teachers, supervisors, co-workers, preachers, and a host of acquaintances... All of these gave a bit of themselves to Pitter-Patt as she tried to give back a bit of herself. The woman was weeping now as her sleep was interrupted once more...

Standing on a beach, "Why in the world am I on a beach", thought Pitter-Pat. "I don't like water and sand". Then, in the distance, Pitter-Patt could see a man lifting something from the beach and tossing it into the water. Walking over for a closer look, Pitter-Patt called to the man, "I know you....you are the man in the story about the star fish"... As she approached the man, Pitter-Patt could see dozens and dozens of star fish had washed upon the beach, and this man was picking them up, one by one, and tossing them back to the safety of the sea... "You have been doing this for such a long time, and still there are thousands that are lying on the sand dying... You can't save them all... so what difference are you making..." To this, the man answered, "I am making a difference for this one", and threw another star fish back into the water. Pitter-pat paused to contemplate the man's words...

There in that place between wakefulness and sleep, Pitter-Patt was enveloped in the sweet aroma of her memories, and pondering the last scene... As with anything after being washed by a flood, the woman felt a sense of "clean"—a sense of renewal. The woman had been given the revelation that her life was worth something—a rich life indeed. God had brought wonderfully common, ordinary people into Pitter-Patt's life to enrich it and bless it. These ordinary people, going about doing ordinary things, yet making an extraordinary difference in one woman's life. As the sun was setting on the horizon, the woman noticed the prisms hanging in the window were creating bright little rainbows across the room. Pitter-Patt smiled and spoke softly—"Thank you, dear Lord in Heaven, for my precious wonderful memories... Thank you, Heavenly Father, for loving me so much to bring such kind and generous people to me... Please, dear God, I pray I can make a difference for those lives I touched... Make my life a sweet aroma to you, Lord, as I strive to give back to you through your people... I can't save them all, but I can make a difference for some—even one... and when my life on earth is over, may I be a blessing and a fond memory for someone... Thank you, Jehovah——..........."

In the midst of her prayer and reverie, Pitter-Patt heard the door open and shut, the sound of feet, and the sweet voice of a child calling, "Auntie Pitter-Patt, where are you".... At that, the woman, misshapen and crooked, got up and set about to fulfill the plan God had for her............ Finishing her prayer, Patter-Pat whispered, "Yes, Lord.... I can make a difference for this one...."

I will lift up mine eyes unto the hills,
from whence cometh my help.
My help cometh from the LORD,
which made heaven and earth.
~ Pslam 121:1-2 ~

Meditation 13:

DEAR LORD...

Dear Lord.....

Oh Lord, God of Heaven...the great and awesome God, who keeps His covenants of love with those who love Him and obey His commands... let your ear be attentive to hear the prayer of your servant.... I come to you in humility and meekness, Father... my heart so laden with the burdens of concern.... Hear me out, Father, and quiet my soul...

Father, my heart cries out for your church. The people are going in all directions and seem scattered like sheep without a strong shepherd. Each is off to see to his own agenda, chasing after dragonflies —they light for a brief time and then fly in every direction... There is a shepherd—he stands at the lead of the flock, Father, but he has a weak voice, and the sheep don't listen.... He is a young shepherd.... He needs time to grow a beard of wisdom and experience, Father... But, for now he seems to need a strong helper to call the sheep together. Instead of being responsible for the leading, he needs a strong teacher to show him the way to lead ... He needs a strong mentor to help this young shepherd to learn about tending the sheep before he will ever be effective as a leader... He needs to learn to nurture the souls, to see to the sick and needy, to be forthright with compassion and concern... He needs to learn how to present himself as the spokesman of your church, conducting himself with the utmost honor and integrity... After all, he is the visible representation of you... The young shepherd can recite scripture, put together a lesson with notes and quips, and even a joke... but Father, there is so much more to it than finding scriptures to suit a phrase, dissecting a word for it's origin, or adding flashy anecdotes .... Father, a good shepherd needs to feed the sheep and protect them... Feed them spiritual food that will sustain them through the days ahead until they come together again at the appointed time... A good shepherd offers protection that will keep the sheep from being devoured by the wolves of satan... but then, I think of Miriam.... Am I a "Miriam" too?... Dare I speak against God's spokesman?... Has the leprosy already eaten away at my heart?... Father, heal my soul....

When I walk into the worship area, there is a coldness about it... cold meeting place... cold eyes... cold words... cold hearts... Are the hearts cold, Father, or is it me who has gone cold?... The worship place is empty, Father... empty seats... empty eyes... empty greetings... empty souls... or, is it me who is empty?... I used to be so full... My heart would heave a sigh of peace at just entering the place of worship—for I was in my refuge once again—my place to rest and be refreshed... Now, I leave still hungering... still seeking that oasis that I once knew... Has your spirit left this assembly... Has your spirit left me..... Father, I see needs being ignored... the poor widow rebuked for asking for help... "You should manage better", she is told... I see the struggler cast aside with a quick, icy "keep trying"... Some have been stricken with devastating sickness... They were left to themselves to get through it... no visits... no notes... no personal words of encouragement... Those few blessed with healing returned to the assembly to be told "we prayed for you"—at which the member would reply, "I didn't know"... Father, you instructed us to come together and pray over the sick... But the sick are ignored.... The struggler is left on the side like an unwanted beggar... We used to reach out to the entire community... Now we reach out to only the favored few... We used to stand firm on truth... We used to shun evil—even the appearance of it... Now, the people seem to chase after whomever would agree with them, neglecting whether they are seeking truth or answering the call of sin.. ... They follow after those who will join in all the frolicking...

no matter that there were sinful, wicked words on the lips of those who now are greeted with the warmth of a friend... No matter at one time those who laugh and sing together with us now once sought to destroy our very existence... But they come now with open invitation—and no mention of a repentance... It's all there now—right there among us—adultery, coveting, pride, greed, pre-eminence, persecution, division... The strong are gathered together in a tight circle while the weak are left outside.... Agree with them, and do as they say—then you will be granted the status of a friend... Dare to question... or far worse—disagree—and you are out... We are to be an "assembly" of people—not individuals... Why then are not all the members informed of the important things going on within the body... Some are left to hear from outsiders who know so much more about "family" business than they ought... We used to be known throughout the community as a church of caring people... Our place of worship used to beckon to the wayward pilgrim, "Come, let us warm your body and feed your spirit"... Now outsiders say, "where is your church? Where are all the caring people"... Chasing after those who will agree and flatter... Chasing after more money to brag about... Chasing after fireflies.... A little glitter and glory for here and now......

I tried to speak out, Father, in a plea for understanding... "Help me to understand why we are straying from the path that once our assembly was on... I can't see that we are still there"... But my questioning was met with rebuke... Was I really out of line with my questions and comments—forgive me Father if I was... Open my eyes to see the wrong in me... Father, you taught us through your word to be a loving people... worn out yet working... tired yet serving... poor, yet giving.... I was that... I worked beyond my weariness... I gave in my poverty... I gave in my prosperity... I served beyond tiredness... Now, time has taken its toll, and my body cannot serve as it once did... Age, illness, and circumstance does not allow me to be as active as I used to be... yet, Father, I am not used up... I still have a place in the assembly... Don't I?.... My heart tells me I must continue to speak out for righteousness' sake... I must continue to serve from where I am now... I still count... Don't I?... Feed my spirit Father... Heal my soul... Light the fire of holy heartburn within me... Help me in my unbelief, Father... Replenish my faith in you, and reconcile my trust in your church...

Lord God Almighty, forgive this sinner... Forgive your people... Set us right again... Fill me with your spirit... Fill you assembly with your spirit... Remember us with kindness and mercy.... Please, God in heaven — — protect and strengthen your people... Protect and strengthen your holy church... I bow before you in humility, offering up honor and praise, and ask that you spare us if only for the righteous few... Please don't remove your lamp stand from us, Father... Please don't remove your holy light and holy spirit from here.......... Holy is your name... Forgiveness and restoration comes from only you... Bestow mercy and grace upon this insignificant child who loves and serves you through your people — bestow mercy and grace upon your holy church here in Corinth.............

*Take my yoke upon you, and learn of me; for I am meek
and lowly in heart: and ye shall find rest unto your souls.
For my yoke is easy, and my burden is light.*
~Matthew 11:29-30~

Meditation 14:

READ THE LABEL

Labels… There are all kinds of labels—labels that warn of danger, labels that describe how to use the product, labels that list ingredients, labels identifying the maker…. How many times have you looked at the label of an item only to see that it was made in some 3rd-world country? So often, this means poor quality of craftsmanship—the fit is wrong, it is so heavy it can't be handled, so light that just looking at it makes it break, inferior or dangerous products used in the make-up… One is hard pressed to find any product that boasts made by human hands with fine craftsmanship. But when you do find one, you can be sure it is of highest quality.

When I was young I was supposed to wear the label "rebellious teen"… that was the go. That was what the "cool kids" labeled themselves and the yoke my age demanded to be accepted by my peers. But that yoke they tried to put on me chaffed and rubbed—it just didn't fit. At first I didn't say anything. When I left the house I put the yoke on before encountering my comrades. And, the yoke came off before entering the house at end of day. I loved my parents, my family… and I enjoyed being with them. I respected and obeyed them. Soon I just gave up this yoke only to have my teen friends put on me another yoke labeled "geek,".

Then I became a "born again" Christian. Another label… another yoke… "Don't listen to music—it belongs to the devil," they said… "Don't wear make-up or fancy clothes," they said…."Sing only songs of struggle and persecution," they said... "Spend all your waking hours reading and praying..." The yoke rubbed, and chaffed and was so heavy, and took away the joy of life itself. Here again, I would take off this yoke in the confines of my home. This yoke just didn't fit. After some time, it was replaced by the yoke labeled "guilt".... "Be popular—throw out a cuss word here/there—grumble about the boss—grumble about the co-workers who weren't around—read the trashy romance novels".... The cuss words left a bad taste in my mouth even though infrequently said. My grandma would be so disappointed to hear words like that coming from me! The boss was fair towards me... the co-workers were kind and friendly... I had no reason to grumble. The novels passed on to me for my turn to read caused my face to turn red. The intricate details of what should be kept private in the bedroom burned my eyes to read and tainted my brain. After receiving only a couple—"Enough!", says I. How could nice people read such smut and encourage others to do the same, and encourage people to continue to write and sell such garbage!?! My language cleaned up, my appreciation for my job, my boss, and my co-workers was demonstrated, and the books were returned, unread, with a request to take me off their round-robin list of sharing. Oh, this yoke definitely did not fit. It was quickly replaced with the yoke of "loneliness"........

A new label, a new yoke surfaced as I was trying to find my way. This time the label came with a Bible, some hugs, and lots of friendly people. That "born-again" era was just a prelude to the real thing. We found our church home, and I found new purpose to my life. But along with this renewed life came a new yoke. This time the fashion of it came with good instructions—read your Bible, pray often, go to worship service and studies, reach out to others. But it came with extra "fine print" attached.... Forsake family for church family. I missed out on some important family time. Even so, my family loved me and tolerated my insistence to be at church rather with them. I was leaving them in the dark—literally. "You must be married...find a good Christian man and set your sites to grab him, for only through marriage are you truly fulfilled"..."If you love the Lord you will forsake everything and everyone, living destitute like a penny-pinching miser, and be a carbon-copy of your religious family":... I was so desperate to fit into this yoke, so desperate to fit the mold. One night I just cried, "Oh, Lord, this yoke doesn't feel right. Who would show my loved ones your love and forgiveness... how can I hurt them by neglecting them.... How is that going to show them the way to find a relationship with you... My family needs me, Lord.... I need my family... As for marriage—that is in your hands, Lord, according to your plan for me... You can fulfill me with your love and purpose... I just can't conform to a mold like the others.... This new yoke is unsettling and hurts—hurts me, hurts others... Lord, if this is your yoke for me, please help me to fit into it better"....

Remember reading in history and storybooks about the yoke put on the oxen? The good owner would make sure the yoke fit the oxen properly, not chaffing or causing pain or discomfort. The yoke must have a good fit in order for the animals to do what was expected of them. The Bible speaks of yokes too. Jesus even offers, "Take my yoke upon you, and learn from me for I am gentle .... My yoke is easy and my burden is light"...[Matthew 11:29-30] The yoke made by Jesus would have a perfect fit—smooth and just right. Many a clergymen and other religious ones are so quick to put yokes on their followers —the yoke of segregated worship halls, women shouldn't cut their hair, fasting before worship service, pray to the east, pray to the sun, cover your head, cover your face, kneel when speaking God's name, use a piano in worship, use a band, use only human voices, don't eat meat, don't eat cows, don't seek medical help from physicians, sickness and disease are punishment for sin, feeling guilty all the time is good.... On and on and on..... Every home has a closet_filled with various yokes to be taken out and put on before stepping out the door—even back in Israel. The high priests and scribes of Israel had so many yokes they put upon the people... Don't talk to Samaritans... Don't work on the Sabbath... Don't go near the sick... Don't associate with sinners or gentiles... Don't eat unclean animals... Every one stamped with *"made by Pharisees"*. Then Jesus came along like a traveling salesman, bidding people to try the yokes carved and crafted by Him according to His Father's instruction. For those who took Him at His offer, they found new freedom and comfort, and a more perfect way to work together.

Where would the Samaritan woman of John 4 be if Jesus had not taken off the Pharisees' yoke and spoke words of life to her? Where would the man with the shriveled, useless hand be if Jesus had kept on the yoke of keeping the Sabbath and let the man remain disfigured? Where would the sinner be if Jesus had not set aside the Pharisee's yoke and gone to take a meal with that old tax collector? (Who, by the way, later wrote one of the gospels).... And the disciples— they were starving when Jesus took off the yoke of tradition and instructed them to eat the grain heads, to worry not about washing hands and utensils, or what day of the week it was.

Now, sound doctrine is not the same thing as these burden-some yokes. Sound doctrine built on the foundation of God's holy word is made to guide, instruct, comfort, and give freedom from sin and guilt—to live in close communion with Him. These burden-some yokes are formed from man grasping bits of scripture from its context and shaping it to fit his own purpose. Most are made to rule over people. But the yoke made by Jesus is fashioned for each individual to fit his needs perfectly. There it was.... The person isn't made to fit the yoke—the yoke is made to fit the person. Finally I understood, and I learned how to pick and choose according to God's will. My family is important. I need to be there for them, to show them the love of God. I need to be a visible representation of Christ to them as they have been to me. They have given so much to me, and I need to give back to them. His yoke has helped me to do that. The yoke of Jesus has helped me to find balance in my life, to live for Him according to His standard—not the standard made up by someone else. The yoke of Jesus doesn't chaff, rub or leave painful imprints. Instead, His holy yoke fits like a warm coat, tailor-made and wraps around to offer security, peace and guidance. Burdens were lifted when I slipped into Jesus' yoke. His yoke led me to understand myself, and who I am, to let go of guilt and shame and bask in His forgiveness, to seek His will for me, to hunger for God's word, to know my purposes here on earth—and to work to fulfill them. *"Take my yoke upon you, and learn from me for I am gentle .... My yoke is easy and my burden is light"*... (Matthew 11:29-30) Why would anyone not chose the yoke made by Jesus... After all—He was a carpenter wasn't He....

"The Lord is about to pass by.... the Lord was not in the wind... the Lord was not in the earthquake... the Lord was not in the fire... after the fire came a gentle whisper...."
~1 Kings 19:11-13 [NIV]~

Meditation 15:

CANT' I HAVE PEACE?

"Can't you leave me at peace?!!?", I said as I felt that long nose nudge me for the third time. It was the dog wanting attention again, and I just didn't feel like being bothered by a mangy mutt right now. As I was about to shoo her away, I looked up from the task I was doing to look into the soft brown eyes of an adoring pet... and at the drooling smile of a baby in her walker with her three brand new teeth glistening back at me. My disposition had been icy for some time, and the sight of these two seemed to melt the coldness encroaching on my heart. The world was put outside, the work was left unfinished, and I went to receive the love and blessings offered by this unlikely pair that I almost shrugged off... and I so desperately needed.

Ever have a period in your life when you feel miserable and just want to stay in it? I mean, you know it's not right... it's not healthy... it's not where you want to be... but there you are all the same. You don't know how you got there, but there you be.... and there you stay because right now everything and everyone is an irritant and you just want to be left to wallow in the misery. That's where I was for a lot of days... Misery Island. It's an island, you see, because you are isolated there... all alone there... and that's the way you like it... and want to keep it... at least for a while.

Well, that day when the "Sunshine Duo" came along to bring me back to the mainland, I recognized that the founder of my misery island was Satan. I guess I knew that all along, but just didn't even want to fight back at that either. The darkness faded a bit and I started to reach for the sun... and the SON. It wasn't mystical how Satan and his evil henchmen got such a hold on me. I had not been spending time in God's word as much in the days just before this all began. I was so busy doing for the Lord that I forgot to spend time with Him. Energy was zapped, emotions were frayed, and resistance was weak. The old devil even invaded my sleep with wicked dreams so there was no getting away from him. Prayers were scanty and sparse. When disappointing news came one day, I felt to blame for it. I had not prayed for the situation as I had promised. Loved ones were counting on me to be in league with them praying fervently for their cause... and I had let them down. There I was off on the sea of guilt. "People were counting on you to pray for this, and you let them down" was what I heard the devil whisper in my ear. "They trusted you to petition the Father on their behalf... and you didn't do that enough." I wanted to cry at every turn of each day, but the tears wouldn't come. A dry desert was what my heart felt like.

Then I looked into the eyes of a baby and a dog... I heard the squeals of a 6-yr-old at the sight of the pumpkin she was harvesting... I heard the gentle voice of my Father calling me to come out of the darkness and back into the Light. In that voice I heard Him remind me to not ignore or reject His blessings around me. In that voice I heard *"Know that I am your God and I will not forsake you nor leave you"*. In that voice I heard all the love and mercy and forgiveness that has been handed from the garden all the way down to me. I was reading again... I was in conversations with my God throughout the day... I found little sprits of solitude to meditate on His goodness and grace... the days were brighter than before... the cold grip on my soul was loosening... though still parched in places, the desert was receiving water again. Satan is constantly, continually pecking away at my countenance, and I must keep my armor in place to protect the fragile soul within. A few small battles have been won, but the war is still raging.

Instincts tell me to keep all this pent up inside. But, this experience was not unique to me, I fear. And I imagine that each one has either been in this dark place before, or will someday be there too.

It comes to every Christian at some point in his/her walk. Don't think yourself odd... or weak-spirited, my friend. The dark places in our lives are not the totality of our lives. Nor, should they be the focus. Instead, the coming back, the victory over them is the story to proclaim. Thank God for the lifeline that is tied around each believer's soul. And, when you feel yourself going down for the third time, don't look for God to come in the wind or the fire or the earth shaking. Listen for His gentle voice... look for Him in the simple blessings around you. Hold still and feel Him embrace you and pull you back to Him. God has granted us to be equipped for the battles... if only we would take advantage of the opportunities He brings through Bible reading, studies, Christian fellowship, and meditation with Him. When the darkness falls around and shrouds you, hold tight to your God... even when everything in you is apathetic and lethargic. Hold tight to that thread of Life that will bring you back to the safety of the Father's embrace. And, when all seems bleak and lost... and the night seems to never end... Hold on my child... joy comes in the morning. Friday was black... Ah... but then came bright and beautiful Sunday....

God be with you and strengthen you.................

But when he was yet a great way off,
his father saw him, and had compassion, and ran,
and fell on his neck, and kissed him.
~Luke 15:20~

SAFE IN DADDY"S ARMS

As she sat there on the pew in that no-where place between sleep and wakefulness, her eyes searched for something familiar—someone familiar. And then... there he was —Daddy. He scooped her up into his arms and she nestled into his neck taking in the comfort of being somewhere she felt secure... Daddy's arms. What a blessed place to be... in the comfort and security of a familiar presence.

I remember my daddy's arms. They were strong arms that were strong enough to lift a ton or gentle enough to set a baby bird back into the nest. Dad was not afraid to roll up his sleeves and put those arms to work. Within the circle of my dad's arms we found direction, comfort, praise, security, and love. Everyone respected Dad—especially his family. Eldest granddaughter, Cindy, lovingly called him "Dumps", and named her puppy after him. Cindy learned compassion from her grandpa. Michael wanted to be like grandpa. At grandpa's funeral Michael made the statement, "Grandpa didn't say much, but when he did—you listened". Michael learned to give an honest day's work from his grandpa. Heather kept her grandpa company on the long journeys across the state when he would transport them to us for the summer. Didn't matter that she was only a toddler at the time, and they were traveling at night. She stayed awake with him all the way. Heather learned to seek direction from her grandpa. Virginia learned to skip from her grandpa. He took her out and patiently skipped down the road with her until she caught on. Virginia learned diligence from her grandpa. James is grandpa's namesake. The boy is built like his grandpa from his long legs to his slender fingers. James learned the importance of heritage from his grandpa. Melanie had a way with her grandpa. She must have—otherwise why would we find him sitting at the kitchen table at 6 AM playing "Go Fish" with her. Melanie learned to find joy in the small things from her grandpa. Joseph was grandpa's soul mate. They spent hours together in grandpa's tool shed. Joe got his own set of tools the day grandpa found all the screwdrivers pounded into the dirt. Joe learned responsibility from his grandpa. The great-grandchildren felt grandpa's arms as well. Although he was only here for the arrival of the first few, he loves them all and lives within each one. They are learning the importance of family from the great-grandpa they know only from pictures and stories. Dad took his arms, formed a circle around my mom and their offspring, and made for us a warm place to go that the world can't destroy. He made a family with roots that run deep. And even now, from Heaven, we can feel Dad's loving arms coaxing us on in the direction that will lead us to be with him again one day.

The story of the prodigal son is a favorite of Bible readers because we all like a happy ending... and a second chance. (In fact, someone wrote a song not so long ago with this very theme.) The son gets his head up thinking in youthful arrogance that he knows better what he needs; and in his wake of leaving, leaves behind a broken-hearted father who only wanted the best for his beloved child. Picture the father pacing back and forth each day, searching the horizon for a glimpse of his missing child coming home. Imagine the restless nights as the father lies on his bed, eyes wide open staring into the dark, thinking of where his child could be... is he safe... is he cared for... is he ever coming home... Night after night the scene is the same —father agonizing over the son's foolish decision that would only lead to pain and destruction for his child. (Notice the father didn't go in search of the child or demand him to come home) And, then... one day... there he is... the child is coming down the road toward home. The look that greeted the child wasn't one of disgust or rejection... but it was the

look of love and relief on the father's face. The son might say...
*"...The day I left home, I knew I'd broken his heart; I wondered
if things would ever be the same... Then one night, I remembered
his love for me; and down that dusty road, ahead, I could see it...
the only time, the only time I ever saw him run was when he ran to
me; took me in his arms, held my head to his chest, and said "My
son's come home again. Looked in my face, wiped the tears from
my eyes, with forgiveness in his voice he said, "Son, do you know
I still love you?"...* (Written by Benny Hester) Do you think that
child ever refused to do the father's bidding from that day on? Do
you suppose that child ever ceased from doing his utmost to live
in such a way that would please the one who never gave up on
him? Do you suppose that child, who was once living in despair
and loneliness, ever forgot the warm feeling of being back in the
secure presence of someone who would always love him... the love
in the eyes, the tenderness in the voice, the encouragement in the
words the father spoke as he urged his son to rebuild his life on the
solid foundation of the father's love? The son who was lost now
was back in the father's care. (Luke 15:20-24)

The parable of the prodigal son isn't so much a story of a lost
son, but more a story of a father's love. It's a picture of the relationship between mankind (the lost and rebellious children) and God
(the Loving Father). The Father sits with a tear in His eye as man,
His beloved creation, goes about willfully doing all that leads to
destruction—man's own destruction. The Father sits fidgeting on
His Throne as man cries out in loneliness and pain —but doesn't
reach for the consoling of his Maker. The Father shakes His head
in disappointment and whispers to Himself..." I made you for better
things than this"... Ah, can't you see the richness of life I offer you...
If only you would come back to Me........" That's the story of you
and me. We were once rebellious children living away from the
Father, and living contrary to the Father. But His love kept reaching
out, calling us back Home. And then one day, in despair and desolation, the rebellious heart is pricked, the clutter is removed from the
self-willed mind, and the way Home is clear. There is an urgency to
turn away from the shabby, dirty, frightful life and get back to the
safety found in the Father's embrace. And, as you and I cry, *"Father,*

forgive me"... and softly sob into His chest, we nestle into that warm security of His love, we feel His mercy and grace envelope us, and hear the forgiveness in His voice as He whispers, *"Child, I am here, and I still love you..."* What a blessed place to be.... in our Father's arms...............

But Mary kept all these things,
and pondered them in her heart.
~ Luke 2:19 ~

I LOVE YOU, MOMMY

"Every mother has a treasure box of bonnets, blankets, and toys and, if not hidden in a closet or an attic, then tucked away in a corner of her heart;" (taken from *"Mary's Treasure Box"*, by Carlyn Walz Kramlich)

Every mother nearly bursts with love at the sound of her child uttering, "I love you Mommy". God created the heart of a servant and placed it in a vessel named "Mother". A mother gives of herself to her child, seeing to every need, seeking only the best for her children. A mother nurtures instincts in the child to grow into a responsible member in the world's circle of humanity. She teaches, preaches, scolds, hugs, praises, provokes, loves. A mother sets aside her own ambitions to see to her child. She lays down her life for the sake of the child. That was God's intention when He created mothers.

The Bible is a record of mothers, good and bad. In Genesis, the first mother, Eve, comes to us. Adam named her "Eve", meaning "mother of all the living". Also, in Genesis, we find Rebecca, who favored one son over the other, and even devised a method to see that her favored son received a blessing that was not rightfully his. Then there is the mother written of in Revelation. This "Jezebel" taught her children to be instruments of lewd wickedness. But there in the midsection is the mention of a sweet young mother, Mary, who brought the Savior into the world. Also, there is mention of Eunice. This woman was praised for the faith she taught her son, Timothy.

But the mother who interests me most is *my* mother. Although her name will probably never be in books or songs, she holds a place of distinction in the community of people known as her family.

Mom is a walking, talking hospitality unit. As far back as I can remember, there was always a big proverbial "Welcome" sign hanging above our door. Anyone who entered knew in an instant that this woman was ready to serve. A cool cup of water or hot cup of coffee, a bandage for a skinned knee, a brief respite for a frazzled soul, a laugh, a tear, a word of encouragement, a smile, a hug—all, and even more are found in my mom's house and heart. The Statue of Liberty boasts, "....*Give me your tired, your poor, your huddled masses yearning to breathe free, the wretched refuse of your teeming shore. Send these, the homeless, tempest-tossed to me, I lift my lamp beside the golden door! ...*". But "Lady Liberty" has nothing over my mom. Hands calloused from hot water and hard work could so gently caress a sobbing soul, pick up the broken pieces of a dream, and set the world right again.

There are so many hours spent sitting in doctors' offices that we can't count them. Most were for me due to my illness that hit at a young age. While others complained and just made everyone around them miserable, my mom would simply sit and wait. She would listen carefully and follow every order from the doctor. It didn't matter that so often it would require so much effort from my mom to accomplish what the doctors asked. "Try to get this awful medicine into her", they would say. Mom would try patiently for hours to coax me to swallow the horrid stuff. "Exercise her joints and muscles several times a day", they would say. Mom would cry right along with me, but we did it all the same. "Keep her in the whirlpool for at least 30 minutes", they would say. If it had not been for my mom's strong hold, I would have surely floated away down the drain in that rush of water and bubbles. Through all the surgeries, many hours of therapies, and long hours of waiting for it to get better, Mom was always there offering hope for a better day.

Mom never grew tired of enjoying the simple pleasures life offered She finds tremendous delight in a conversation with a three-year-old great-grandchild, or in sharing a bowl of popcorn with a sixty-two-year-old son Mom loves a good story, especially one on herself. Her favorite fish story is to tell of her biggest catch—my younger brother. Mom thought she was casting the fish line out into the lake. Instead she cast it right into the cheek of my younger brother. Needless to say, we ended that fishing trip in the local emergency room. She also tells the tale of her famous "secret recipe" for French-fried potatoes. While adding more oil to the kettle, she accidentally poured honey into the pot instead. One day Mom set a plate of chicken aside for another meal—she was expecting company. Now she laughs while telling of her surprise when she went to retrieve the chicken to prepare the meal only to find that plate empty. A hungry son had wandered through the kitchen earlier. Mom lovingly recounts the stories of her younger days. We sit at her feet and listen to when our dad moved Mom away from the farm he loved because she didn't like farming. We smile as she remembers how her brothers helped with her chores so she could come play softball with them because she was their best pitcher. We would nod in agreement as she would recall the times my grandparents on both sides lived with us. We would cry along as she told of the hard times, and laugh as she would tell of the happier days.

Faith. Mom always has had a strong faith in God, and a certainty that He was always near, watching over her family. Now, in the later years when family demands are not so many, Mom has been able to involve herself in more formal church-based activities. But always did she hold fast to the truth that there is a necessity for a relationship with Almighty God, and the importance of prayer. God knew I would need a mother with a gentle spirit, patient, kind, diligent, loving. He gave me *"Mom"*. Others may tire of a routine like ours. Many grow weary after only a few days of such physical demands. But my mom never gives up. Even through her own sicknesses, she still tends to my needs unfailingly. It amazes me the way Mom comes into me each morning dressed in a smile and a prayer ready to meet the demands and blessings of the day. I see in my mother the character of Christ.

The strongest impression from my mother has been her self-sacrifice. Mom literally gave me her blood when doctors transfused blood products taken from my mom and put them into my disease-ravaged body. She gives so much of herself to family and friends.

She never grows weary of giving her time and energy to those around her who needed her. She is the light of our household—a household knit together by the love and devotion she gives so generously. Mom could have had fine features and an elegant appearance. Instead of spending time primping on herself, she was helping us with homework. Mom could have been a member of any number of social groups. Instead, she was a scout leader, a classroom mom, a cheerleader at little league ballgames. Mom could have supped on crustless sandwiches and drunk tea from dainty cups and saucers. Instead, she spent her time making a snack for her husband at midnight after he came home from his second- or third job; or she made tomato soup at 6 AM for a sick child; or worked at stretching a package of hamburger to feed a house-full of church visitors. Mom is not perfect. She gets angry, she yells when she might have remained silent, she keeps a confusing ledger in her checkbook.... In all her imperfections, Mom did one thing definitely right in her life—she married our dad! God put His finger on Mary to be the mother of the Lamb of God. God put His holy finger on this woman to be the mother of the insignificant souls who call her blessed. The woman of Proverbs 31 we call *"Mom"*.

I pray that He will bless me to learn from my mom, to glean her wisdom, goodness, and godliness, and put it to work in and through my life. I pray that I may be a reflection of the Christ I see in my mother. And, as my mother tucks away those precious things into her treasure box, may it be overflowing with love and appreciation from her family. Please, dear Lord, let me be a blessing for my mom as she has been such a rich blessing for me. *I love you, Mom.*

*For I reckon that the sufferings of this present time
are not worthy to be compared with the glory
which shall be revealed in us.*
~ Romans 8:18 ~

BLESS THE HARD TIMES

So often the question is asked, "why must there be so much suffering, pain, and hurt?" "Why must life be so hard some times"? John Bunyan addressed these questions in his story, "Pilgrim's Progress". Mr. Bunyan writes, "What must we do in this holy place?, asked the pilgrims. The answer came, "You must there receive the comforts of all your toil and have joy for all your sorrow; you must reap what you have sown, even the fruit of all your prayers and tears and sufferings for the King throughout your pilgrimage" Yes, Mr. Bunyan, but it's so hard. So much seems impossible to overcome. Why must we suffer? Why must the innocent suffer? The answer is simply stated. Sin. Sin came into the world and brought pain, crying and death with it. But, we aren't left in the storm of sin to live there forever. There is a rainbow that follows the storm if we but have an eye to see.

Hermit crabs are one of the smallest marvels of God's creation and live in a seashell with only their heads and legs sticking out. All that you really see is a shell with legs that occasionally carry it around. The little crabs come out of their shells on only two occasions—first, when the crab is molting and growing; the other when he is experiencing stress. Wait a minute. There are times when I have experienced stress that was allowed by God Like the crab, I needed to come out of my shell and grow. My comfort zones, my boundaries, my self-imposed limitations needed to change. God was allowing the stress in my life so I would deepen my relationship with Him. It's never comfortable. But, I have found that when I shed this shell that is too small, God always moves me to a bigger place in my life. Most of the great truths of God have been learned during difficult times. Ask Job.

In the first two chapters of the book of Job, God gives a look behind the scenes so that the reader can watch from Heaven's viewpoint as the events take place on earth. There is no doubt that if Job could have seen into the councils of heaven before and during his trials, he would have handled it all differently. But God did not allow Job that insider information, nor did God explain it at the close of his experience. Job may have learned about the details after he arrived in Heaven, but not before. God's eternal purpose for Job would have been thwarted had Job been given the explanation up front for his trials. If Job had known all that took place in Heaven regarding him, there would have been no place for faith. Without faith, the Hebrew writer says it is impossible to please God. Job could never have been purified, as gold is purified with fire, had he not gone through the situation in which he had to trust God completely. God has permitted us to see these things in order to help strengthen our faith when it comes to facing baffling afflictions. His purpose is that we might place complete trust and faith in Him, believing that the hard experiences in life are permitted to fulfill a greater purpose.

We need to learn to praise the Lord as much for the closed doors we do for the open ones. The reason God closes doors is because He has not prepared anything over there for us. If the wrong door had not been closed to us, we would never find the right door. God directs our path through the closing and opening of doors. We can sometimes trap ourselves in doubt and discouragement through judging by appearances instead of trusting God to give us all we need just at the time we need it. This is true in both blessings and trials. We must learn to fix our eyes upon Him and trust. God closes a door just to open another in unexpected places. Sometimes in the belly of a great fish is just where we need to be in order to remember to heed His calling. Sometimes down in the valley we will feel the warmth of his love most. Ask God to give you the back to bear the burden He chooses to give you—and give Him glory for it. Accept

God's will to be placed either on the mountaintop or in the valley, in good times and tribulation.

Sometimes the struggles come not so much for the believer's learning, but for those spectators around the believer. Shortly after our family had gone through the death of my father, and some other family issues, my friend and I were out on our daily walk. This friend knew of the trials our family was experiencing and commented to me, "I don't know how you can keep going, day after day—and keep smiling". This gave me an open door to tell her how God was sustaining us, how He was strengthening us, and bringing us through. It gave me an opportunity to testify to the comfort and peace that comes with trusting in the promises of God. Little did either of us know that this conversation was a prelude, a preparation for what was a head. God was preparing both of us for the time when she would need me to help her walk the last struggle of her life—and help me to let her go. God truly does give us what we need before we know we need it.

There are times we struggle with feelings of loneliness, abandonment or betrayal. There are times we feel so alone, forgotten and unimportant. Jesus went to that place of loneliness so we wouldn't have to live there. He went bearing our sins so that we could be made righteous again. We deserve the stripes He bore. He took our guilt and shame upon Himself and turned it to glory. Ours was a promise of eternity spent in blackness and despair. Jesus became our mediator pleading His blood as an atonement, buying back our promise to spend eternity in the Light of heaven. A member of the Godhead took on the form of man and left heaven to come to earth to suffer and die for a lost world. Why would we not trust that He will work all things for our good. It is during those hard times that we acknowledge our weakness and proclaim our complete dependence upon Almighty God. It's through those times of trails that God can truly make us strong. Through those trials we learn to trust in Jesus, learn to trust in God, learn to depend upon His Word. Think of it—if we had never had a problem, we wouldn't know that God could solve it, we wouldn't know what tremendous things faith in God can do. Once we recognize that we can't even take a step without holding to God's hand, then we will truly learn to walk.

Don't spend precious time pondering the why's and wherefore's of life. Pain and strife are real, no doubt about it. And when the dark demons put their squeeze on our lives, we hurt and sweat and cry. But God is near to the brokenhearted and downtrodden. God is so good to us. God is so good *for* us. Go back to the sea and ponder the starfish. He quietly goes about the work God created him for. The little creature gets caught in a net or a predator's teeth and loses an arm. But God created the starfish to regenerate a replacement. It can suffer a loss, only to pick itself up and carry on, growing and renewing. We can do that too. We can be regenerated by the love and care provided by God. We can take each day as it comes. Despite the weight of the present affliction of this world, make every effort to focus on the positive and good in each day, each moment. Let us embrace the valleys as a gift from the potter to mold and define us into His perfection. Praise him for purging the debris from our souls in order that we might reflect the image of His Son. Let us stand strong on our rock of faith that He will work good out of our trials and bring us from the valley of desolation to the mountain of hope. And there we will live forever with Him.

Before I formed thee in the belly I knew thee;
and before thou camest forth out of the
womb I sanctified thee…
~ Jeremiah 1:5 ~

SNOWFLAKES

Have you ever tried to catch snowflakes on your tongue? Ever tried to make identical cut-out paper snowflakes? Not easy, huh. Ever examine snowflakes and found that each one has its own pattern, and no two are alike? Amazing!

If snowflakes are so amazing with their separate detail, then how about us? There are not two humans who are identical. Each has his/her own individual identity, own character, own soul. Even identical twins have little individual markings that make each a separate entity. Such time, care, and love is spent in creating man. Look at each of us. Not two alike. Some are tall and lanky, while others are short and stout. Some are dark-skinned with dark eyes and dark hair. Some are fair-skinned with blue eyes and light hair. When one of my nephews, Jeremiah, was small, he noticed differences in people. Jeremiah had been playing with a child with dark skin, hair and eyes. As the boy sat coloring a picture, he asked what color his playmate was. With some irritation, his sibling answered him, "You know she is black, and you are white." To this, blue-eyed, blond-haired, six-year-old Jeremiah studied his box of crayons for a bit and replied, "Uhnt-uh…. '*I'm peach*!'"

Go beyond the outward and look at the person inside. Some are boisterous with life seeming to bubble right out. Some are quiet, serious, and subdued. Some live their lives like an open book, while others are more inward keeping feelings deep. But, no matter the differences, God has made each one with a special gift to share and use to the glory and praise of His Kingdom. God told Samuel to go to the house of Jesse and find the next king of Israel. Samuel checked out all the strong, husky lads belonging to Jesse, but came up short of one who measured up. As Samuel cried in despair to God, he was reminded to stop looking at the outward appearance as the world does. Instead look to the person inside. When Samuel looked to the inner person, he found the perfect king for his people—Jesse's youngest son, David. That six-year-old boy, Jeremiah, was gifted with a heart full of compassion and care for others. He looked at people for who they were in their hearts, and he cared about them. He demonstrated that gift all through his short life. And, when God called him Home at age 18, Jeremiah's gift of caring lives on in those who were blessed to be touched by this boy's spirit.

How are you using the gifts God has given you? What?!!?? Was that murmuring and grumbling? "I don't have any gifts or talents", you said? Can you offer a word of encouragement to someone struggling with life? Do you have a spare moment to compliment someone on the fine job he/she is doing? A word of congratulations to a mother on the nice behavior of her young child at worship service? A hug for a soul looking a bit lonely? Time to admire a work of art from a child? A joyful spirit to offer in the song portion of worship so as to encourage the song leader? Undivided attention to the speaker? Maybe your gift is making cookies, or cleaning, or working numbers. Maybe you have broad shoulders and an ear to listen. Maybe you have a depth in Bible knowledge and could share that knowledge with someone struggling to grasp these truths. Maybe yours is the gift of a smile that brightens the room and lightens the load for a few minutes. Whatever your talent, it is a gift from God to be shared.

While we all are made different, we all have one thing in common. We are all made in the likeness of the Lord. God made His people to be one in spirit working as one body, serving one God in one faith. Our nation's pledge of allegiance even understands this concept—"one nation under God..." Our many differences blend together in sweet harmony because of the one cord that runs through all of us—our love for Jesus Christ, the Son, and our devotion to God, the Father.

Getting back to the snowflakes... Have you ever looked over a field of newly fallen snow? You wish that nothing would come to distort its perfect, clean appearance. And, then you run out to cover the field with snow angels. Each new day starts out untouched, waiting for us to make our "snow angels" in it for God's pleasure and glory. Each day is a new opportunity to use our gifts to make a difference for the better in the world around us. Each snowflake falls to earth to join with all the others to cover the land making it clean, white, and pure again. Each time we slip into that old, black pit of sin, the blood of Jesus falls upon us, covering us, making us clean, white and pure again.

Let us look at the box of crayons and remember that we need each and every color to make our world a beautiful place. Black, brown, red, yellow, *peach*—all have an important purpose to fulfill. Let us remember the snowflakes—each different, yet each important to bring beauty to the land. Let us encourage one another to bring all of our diversified abilities together to bring about peace and hope to a world caught in chaos and despair. Let us remember that God created each one, and each is precious in His sight. That includes you and me. *Praise God!*

Be strong in the Lord, and in the strength of his might.
Put on the whole armor of God, that ye may be able to
stand against the wiles of the devil. For our wrestling is
not against flesh and blood, but against the principalities,
against the powers, against the world-rulers of this dark-
ness, against the spiritual hosts of wickedness in the heav-
enly places. Wherefore take up the whole armor of God,
that ye may be able to withstand in the evil day,
and, having done all, to stand.
~Ephesians 6:10-13~

Meditation 20:

SOKDIERS OF CHRIST

R ecently I learned of a unique band of service men (and women).
Members of this military unit stand guard over the tomb of the
unknown soldier in the National Cemetery. Did you know...

They must commit two years of life to guard the tomb, live in
a barracks under the tomb, and cannot drink any alcohol on or off
duty for the rest of their lives. They cannot swear in public for the
rest of their lives and cannot disgrace the uniform or the tomb in
any way. After two years, the guard is given a wreath pin that is
worn on his/her lapel signifying he/she served as guard of the tomb.
(There are only 400 presently worn.) The guards must obey these
rules for the rest of their lives or give up the wreath pin. The shoes
are specially made with very thick soles to keep the heat and cold
from their feet. There are metal heel plates that extend to the top
of the shoe in order to make the loud click as they come to a halt.
There are no wrinkles, folds or lint on the uniform. Guards dress for
duty in front of a full-length mirror. The first six months of duty a
guard cannot talk to anyone, nor watch TV. All off-duty time is spent
studying the 175 notable people laid to rest in Arlington National
Cemetery. A guard must memorize who they are and where they are
interred. Among the notables are: President Taft, Joe E. Lewis {the
boxer} and Medal-of-Honor winner Audie Murphy, of Hollywood
fame. (The most decorated soldier of WWII) Every guard spends
five hours a day getting his uniforms ready for guard duty.

Another tidbit of information—our US Senate/House took two days off as they couldn't work because of an expected storm... Hurricane Isabelle. On the ABC evening news, it was reported that, because of the dangers from Hurricane Isabelle approaching Washington DC, the military members assigned the duty of guarding the Tomb of the Unknown Soldier were given permission to suspend the assignment. They respectfully declined the offer, "No way, Sir!" Soaked to the skin, marching in the pelting rain of a tropical storm, they said that guarding the Tomb was not just an assignment; it was the highest honor that can be afforded to a serviceperson. The tomb has been patrolled continuously, 24/7, since 1930.

Well... I was impressed when I read all of this. What dedication and commitment to a cause these people believe in. What respect for their position and the dead whom they guard. Then my mind pondered —are such noble characteristics so unusual? Surely not... for we all know of just such men/women of integrity. Sometime in the course of life, one runs into a person serving mankind honorably and nobly... a life living diligently to keep a promise or commitment... living in obedience without question. As Christians, we have a heritage packed full of stalwart souls who lived up to what they believed in. Every chapter in the Bible records a wee band of people gallantly upholding and protecting something precious—a belief and a way of life. We are in awe of men who can make such sacrifices and live so selflessly. But—is it really a sacrifice? When one cares deeply for someone/something, is it a "sacrifice" to give of one's time, energy, and heart? Our greatest example is Jesus Christ, Himself. Did He not offer the Living Water to a woman at a well instead of resting Himself? Did He not patiently offer lesson after lesson to those who wanted to know but just couldn't understand? Did He not set the example of a servant when He washed the feet of His friends? Scripture tells us that Jesus had determined to "sacrifice" for mankind before man was created. He left the riches of Heaven and He would empty Himself—take on the form of a servant to save the creation He loved. His uniform was not pressed with sharp creases, but stained and worn from hours in the sun fulfilling the Promise made to David and Abraham. His shoes were not polished but covered with dust from walking from town to town to bring the Good News to mankind. The call to duty was a high one... the requirements stiff. But Jesus stepped up and answered the call. He took the role of a soldier to fight a holy war against all the powers and demons of darkness. And so did Peter, and John, and James, and Stephen, and Paul. For over 2000 years men have stepped up to the call with humility, honor, and integrity. Through all their efforts these dedicated ones sought only to bring glory to the One Who gave the greatest sacrifice—His Life... and they received the crown of life for their courage, steadfastness, and obedience.

The call is there for anyone—everyone. Love Him so deeply, and His cause, that there would be no request too great to grant. Commit to the cause, live a life worthy to wear the mark of honor, bring no disgrace to the uniform of a Christ-follower, and stand tall for righteousness' sake. No matter what storm wails at us, we will not be moved to leave our post... for our guarding the Tomb is not just an assignment, it is the highest honor that can be afforded to man. Our call is not to guard the tomb of an unknown soldier, but to proclaim to the world that *The Tomb is empty...* this Soldier has claimed victory over the enemy and now sits at the right hand of the King of kings. And, we can too... if we but only take the call seriously, step up to it wholeheartedly in total obedience, willing to set aside anything that hinders from serving in honor, nobility, integrity and love. Soldiers of Christ—Arise!

Give her of the fruit of her hands;
and let her own works praise her in the gates"
~Proverbs 31:31~

Meditation 21:

HANDS

Have you ever looked at hands? Really *looked* at hands? Hands are as unique as the person they are attached to. These appendages are taken for granted, their uses never really appreciated. Let us take a moment to study these marvelous members of our amazing bodies.

Since I was so young when my grandpa died, I don't remember him much except for his hands—big hands that held my tiny ones so lovingly. One of my favorite teachers had hands with long slender fingers. He was our music teacher and played the piano beautifully. The veins in his hands were pronounced, as were the tendons and muscles. I loved my dad's hands. Dad's hands were strong. They were marred and calloused from hard work. Those hands would be grease-covered from repairing a car engine, yet clean enough to help out with supper dishes. They were strong enough to lift twice his weight, yet tender enough to change a grandchild's diaper. Those hands could build a stand for our homemade nativity set, fix a discarded lawnmower and make it run like new, place a baby bird back in its nest, bait a fish hook, play a "Go Fish" card game, push his daughter on the swing, demonstrate how to swing a bat for his son. Hands strong enough to discipline, yet tender enough to clasp his wife's hand in prayer. Dad's hands spoke of an honest day's work, strength, tenderness, love, and integrity. No wonder I loved my dad's hands. I would be remise if I didn't make mention of my mother's hands. These hands also had signs of hard work. Her hands were red from hours in the dishpan, washing clothes, floors, and faces. Yet mom's hands held a storybook as she read to us at rest time, sewed buttons on shirts, made masterpieces out of hamburger, and tucked us in at bedtime. The touch from mom's hands spoke reassurance, security, and love.

Another set of hands I love are the hands of someone who knew hard work. He was a carpenter by trade. His hands built tables and chairs of finest quality. His hands were callused, nails chipped and ragged, veins bulging. Hands of a common laborer. They are wondrous hands that knew no wickedness. These hands touched a blind man and gave him sight. These hands brought life back into a dead body. These hands overturned the tables of the moneychangers and chased their wicked deeds from the holy temple. Wonder after wonder, miracle after miracle, were brought about by these hands. And in deep love and compassion, these hands are outstretched bidding the downtrodden, *"Come unto me, all ye that labor and are heavy laden, and I will give you rest."* (Matthew 11:28)

When one looks at my hands, they see they are small and pudgy, crooked, fragile, and appear quite useless. But these paddles of mine also have a story of love and compassion to tell. These hands have wiped tears from a sorrowful soul, held a baby close rocking it to sleep, scrubbed mud from a small shoe, flicked a bug off a frightened child, penned a note of encouragement, savored the feel of a new crayon, stripped old varnish from a piece of furniture to bring back its original beauty, comforted a crying child as his/her mommy disappeared from sight. These hands can push a vacuum, stir a pot, wipe a dish, and serve a plate of cookies. They can teasingly slug a brother in sibling fun, and stroke the brow of a dying loved one. My debilitated hands may never conduct an orchestra, but they have held a songbook in worship service. My hands may never be strong and beautiful, but they are powerful when clasped together in prayer. Useless hands? Not at all. My hands are not worth much in the world's point of view, but in the Kingdom of God, they are part of His treasure house.

All of these are hands set with strength and power—power in the deeds these hands are capable of. Hands possess the power to steal, to write slanderous words, to hurt, to murder. Or, these same hands possess the power to work good, to help someone in need, write words to encourage and uplift, to offer friendship, comfort and love. These hands can pick up the remote to tune into the world only to be contaminated by its wickedness. Hands are also capable to open the Bible and caress the pages of written scripture preserved through the ages and be transformed into the image of God. Hands able to serve the prince of darkness, or the Prince of Life. Hands have power and strength when joined together in a common cause. But, hands are their most powerful when folded together in prayer. Reach out and join hands with Jesus in the work of the Father. Lift your hands heavenward and feel the enormous power and peace He will give you. As for my hands, I vow here and now to commit my hands to only those things that will bring pleasure, honor, and praise to our Creator. And, one day, my misshapen hands will reach out and touch the face of Jesus.

Wherefore be ye not unwise,
but understanding what the will of the Lord is.
~Ephesians 5:17~

HOLY ROAD MAP

Some years back I became frustrated in my job. I was becoming a disgruntled employee with an attitude not becoming in the least—especially in a person professing to be a Christian. I felt pleased with myself that I always followed God's lead—at least I thought I did. It was evident to me that my work environment was holding me back from being truly great for God. I began to pray, asking God to bring me a new job opportunity, a new place with new people who deserved to hear what I had to say about God, the Father, and Jesus, the Son.

One Sunday while browsing the newspaper, I looked through the classified—something I seldom looked at. There it was leaping from the page. A new job! Quickly, that same day, I polished up the old resume, contacted some generous friends for references, and put this plan into action. After all, wasn't this a concrete sign from God in answer to my prayers. I was off on what I read as a mission from God. That same week an offer came for an interview, and it went beautifully. The benefits were comparable to what I already had, the work was familiar, the compliments were flowing, and the job was offered. My, oh my! My head was swelling with ego and importance. The resignation was beautifully typed and eloquent. I handed out pat answers to co-workers' questions regarding my leaving. "How could I turn my back on a door of opportunity opened by God," I would say. "I was beginning a new phase in my life." "I needed a change."

I felt so positive—and so smug. My work was done in this place. They had rejected my preaching long enough. I was getting out! Farewell Friday came with expressions of encouragement, cards, gifts, and hugs. I accepted it all graciously, but I was off to a better environment. The grass was definitely going to be greener where I was going.

Marvelous Monday came and I was pumped with confidence. I just knew with certainty that I was moving by the hand of God. In my reasoning, I figured God had brought this to me, and I was being obedient by following His lead. It took about two hours for me to realize that this greener grass was not grass at all, but green cement! As the day drew on, my aspirations to set these people on fire faded. That big, delicious carrot the devil hung in front of this donkey's nose was only plastic. So many issues were not right with me being in this new organization. They were tight and cliquey, and turned a nose up at my differences. I had no history with them, and they had no intention of letting me build one. Where I thought I was stepping out in faith like Abraham, to be led by God to a new land, I found I was behaving more like Jonah, refusing to help with the Ninevites. I spent three days in the belly of the great fish all in the span of twelve hours that day. As I sat in my fish's belly, my puffed up ego burst. My self-will was surrendered, my heart was pricked, my eyes opened. Earlier I had prayed that I would be a light to the new ones I would be working with. Instead, *I* found the Light. I turned toward that Light once again, and away from the curtain of flattery that blocked my vision.

God is so good. Let me say it again—*GOD IS SOOOOOO-OOOOOO GOOD*! He let me go just so far and then reeled me back in. Because of His promise to me as His child, God never left me alone to my own devices. What I mistook as God's lead was my own self-will trying to take control of my life when it really isn't my life at all. It is His. God had been shaping and molding me into what He wanted me to be. But, I wanted to try it for a while, so I took it from Him only to drop it with a thud. While I deserved to wallow in my failure and pride, the loving Father picked up the broken pieces and patched my life together again, remolding and reshaping. God moved in such a way during this hard time that I could almost feel

His soothing stroke across my sagging soul. God took this frantic, dismantled being and brought peace and sense back to it. His grace covered me once again. Once I gave control back to God, He gave me back my purpose.

Through grace and mercy on God's part—and my former employer—I was blessed to return to my old job. I was back with the same benefits as when I left, back to the same desk, the same job duties, the same dust bunnies behind my computer, the same co-workers. The same "Ninevites" I turned away from blessed me with a welcome home celebration the prodigal son received. When I thought a change in surroundings was what I needed showed itself to be a change in *me* that was really necessary. I still was met with the same obstacles each day at work, but I had a renewed appreciation for where God had placed me, and a renewed purpose to fulfill _His_ plan for me. My life belonged to Jesus, and I would let Him shine in me and through me in everything I did, whether at work or at leisure.

There was a saying on a desk calendar I had at this time. It read, "The church of Jesus began with a group of frightened men in a second-floor room in Jerusalem. What did Jesus say to them—'what a bunch of flops... I told you so... where were you when I needed you....' No. He said just one phrase. 'Peace be with you'. The very thing they didn't have or deserve was the very thing Jesus offered. Peace." When I was floundering on the brink, God brought His peace to my staggering spirit. My eyes are back on the Creator instead of on the creation. I stopped turning my nose up at those who needed to hear the story of Good News and refused to give an ear. Instead, I would tell them repeatedly, and when they wouldn't listen to my words, I would show them by my life. Since that hard lesson learned, my prayer has been that I may always be ready and willing to allow God to fulfill His divine purpose for me. When the time comes for me to move on, God will bless me with His understanding and His holy map. Until then, I stand firm, right where God planted me.

"Only take heed to thyself, and keep thy soul diligently, lest thou forget the things which thine eyes have seen, and lest they depart from thy heart all the days of thy life: but teach them thy sons, and thy sons' sons..."
~Deuteronomy 4:9~

Meditation 23:

LESSON FROM A LADYBUG

"Ladybug, Ladybug! Run away home! Your house is on fire and your children will burn…" It's a refrain from a silly child's song. But let us put on our news anchorperson hat and look deeper into the story. What was the situation at the time the house was burning? Where was Mrs. Ladybug during the fire? Most likely Mrs. Ladybug was so caught up in what ladybugs do that she didn't even notice that her house and her family were in danger. She no doubt was busy doing good deeds as she always did—checking in on Mr. Cricket's arthritic knees, exchanging the wonders of the garden with Queenie Bee, meeting with Cousin Beetle to share lunch and scripture. All the while she was looking to the needs of others, Mrs. Ladybug's own were going to the wall. Once there was a man who was devoted to his faith and his family. Said the man, "What good are all our efforts to save the world if we lose our own kids in the process?"

Each time I have the special privilege to listen in on the prayers of young ones, I am reminded just how precious and innocent they are. Their hearts are pure and uninhibited. They speak straightforward into the ear of God whatever is on their minds at that moment. A two-year-old says, "Thank you, God, for my mommy". A four-year-old whispers, "Thank you, God, for helping me sleep in my own bed all night by myself". A six-year-old prays in Sunday school, "Dear Heavenly Father, watch over the sick, and those who couldn't come to church today; and, thank you for Jesus". While my heart nearly bursts from emotion over such tender honesty, I am reminded that Satan and his demons of darkness are just waiting for any opportunity to snare, poison, and destroy these sweet souls.

Just what are we willing to do to stop the prince of this world from devouring our children? Just what are we willing to do to protect, instruct, and nurture the future servants of God? Let me suggest that we spend as much time as possible in God's word, gaining wisdom, knowledge, and enlightenment in order that we might impart it to our young ones. May I suggest that we seek opportunities to encourage the young ones around us and get to know them? May I suggest that we be diligent in prayer on behalf of those young souls? Each child has a specific purpose to fulfill in the overall scheme of God's plan for the universe. Each child is especially unique and the only one of his/her kind.

When we look at a bunch of dandelions, we see them as weeds invading our well-groomed lawns. Children see them as flowers for picking, or little launching devices to blow tiny helicopters into the wind. When we see mud puddles, we walk around them avoiding a mess. A child sees the same mud puddle and plots a grand adventure right through it. He envisions dams to build, rivers to cross, and the pure joy of stomping right in the middle of it. When we feel the wind, we grumble about messed hair-do's. Children close their eyes, spread their arms wide, and fly with the wind. We only see the bugs invading our backyard. Children, instead, enjoy the magic show as they watch the fireflies flick bits of sparkle across the evening. When adults hear a favorite song, they dare not hum along for fear of being noticed. Children feel the beat and move with it. They sing along with abandonment—and if they don't know the words, they fill in their own. When adults pray, they use formal words when addressing God, like "*If thou hearest thine servant, and giveth thine blessing....*" Children speak to God as if speaking to a friend—"*Hi God... Thank you for my toys and my mommy and daddy, and sunshine, and the stars, and my dog... and please God, keep the bad dreams away, and help me to be good....*" Let us always live in wonderment at the wonderful gifts God blesses us with, and thank Him as a grateful child. "God bless God", was the close of the prayer of a five-year-old. What about our prayers with God? Do we have something to teach the children—or, do they have a multitude of things to teach us?!!?

Ever ponder the raising of a young David? Or, Daniel? Or, young John, the Baptist? Where do you suppose that spirit of service was nurtured and encouraged? God has placed into our hands the responsibility of raising up the next generation of preachers, teachers, doctors, senators, street-cleaners, babysitters. Let us teach them by example to be compassionate and caring, faithful and honest. Let us share with them an enthusiasm for growing closer to God, and living according to His word. Let us be in constant prayer that we might influence at least one child within our realm to turn away from the glitter in the world, and, instead, give his heart to Jesus. Let us not be guilty of getting so busy in saving the world that we lose those closest to us. Remember to set aside time to feel the joy of a child, and cherish the true gift each child is. For after all, wasn't it our beloved Jesus who said, *"Suffer the little children to come unto me, and forbid them not: for of such is the kingdom of God."* (Mark 10:14) God bless the children everywhere.

"HE heals the brokenhearted
and binds up their wounds..."
~Psalm 147:3~

HOUSE OF HEALING

It was the last thing she had of any true value. It meant the world to her, and her only link to a better life. Yet, as she carried the expensive vessel, she knew this was the right thing to do—the only thing she could do. Shame and guilt had plagued her life for so long. The burden of it weighed so heavy on her. Was it possible that now, at last, there was healing available for her? She would present her exquisite vessel as an offering. Timidly... quietly... she entered the house, and stood off to the side of the group gathered around the table. Single-mindedly she approached the table and sought out her target. Just being in the same room, in His presence, caused the woman to weep. She couldn't hold back her heartache any longer. Tears fell from her eyes upon His feet. Kneeling before Him, she wiped His wet feet with her hair. And then—then, when her heart was bursting with emotion, she was suspended with only she and this one in the room—then, she poured the precious contents of her alabaster jar over His feet. The others scoffed and scolded the woman. "Get out of here...you have no place here with our guests... you are a sinner and have no place among us..." As the woman knelt there, tears still flowing and wiping oil over His feet, Jesus touched her arm and looked tenderly into her eyes. Then, He spoke, "This woman has wet my feet with her tears and wiped them with her hair. She kissed my feet and poured this precious perfume over them. Therefore, her many sins have been forgiven for she demonstrated great love." Placing His hand on the woman's shoulder, He said to her, "Woman, your sins are forgiven. Your faith has saved you. Go in peace". The woman had come to this house guilty, lonely, and broken. The woman left the house forgiven, loved, and whole. This ordinary house, made of mud and straw, had become a holy place invested with the spirit of love and forgiveness—a house of healing. (Taken from Luke 7:36-50)

Walk into a museum, and you immediately sense a respect for the treasures abiding there. Walk into a funeral parlor and immediately sense the reverence for the departed. Walk into a hospital or medical office and sense the seriousness of announcements being made. Walk into a restaurant serving alcoholic beverages and sense lewdness. Walk into a cathedral and sense the sweet aroma of holiness. What makes the difference one might ask? Bricks, granite, mortar, wood, and steel all go into making a building. But, it remains just a building until it is invested with the purpose of it. Sounds and smells make up the atmosphere within the building. The purpose and use of the building makes the distinction. The building used as a place to worship God is invested with His Spirit making it a holy place to meet with the saints. Within the walls of the church's building, souls sit on the pews, smiles painted on the face, but pain and sorrow on the heart. They have been searching for relief from every worldly avenue. Yet all roads lead to this house of God. Inside awaits the balm for the soul. Shattered dreams and broken lives are laid upon the altar. Souls who thought God had abandoned them because they can't feel His presence come in search of something to bring Him back. Clouds of doubt and fear obscure His warmth. Yet, in this holy house, they sit still enough to hear His whisper once more. (Healing.) Walk through the door and sense God's presence. Pause and hear each whispered word. On this Holy Ground there is joy and peace of mind. (Healing.) There is a sweet spirit that comes over each soul and expression of each face. Sometimes there are shouts of "Alleluia". Sometimes "Praise the Lord." Sometimes there's gentle singing. Sometimes, whispered prayers. Sometimes, inward sobs. All come to the feet of Jesus and lay their sins and sorrows, weeping and praying. From

His fullness, they gather blessings of comfort and grace. Each empty vessel is filled. (Healing.)

But it wasn't just in a building that souls met with God. God can invest His holiness into a tent, a campground, a bedroom, a back porch, a barn, a field, a hospital room—wherever His people call upon His name. In 1 Kings 17, we read about the widow of Zarephath. She had opened her house and fed God's prophet, Elijah. Some time later the widow's only son died. Elijah cried to the Lord to revive the boy. In that simple house the boy was restored to his mother. Again in 2 Kings we read of another woman who meets with God's spokesman. This time it is the prophet, Elisha who cries to the Lord on behalf of the Shunammite woman and her son. The breath of life was breathed into the boy and he was restored to his mother. She cried at the feet of the prophet. In Acts 9, there again healing and restoration of life came through the apostle Peter. The story that is so amazing is the account of the centurion. His beloved servant was sick near unto death. When the centurion came upon Jesus, he asked for healing for the servant. "Lord, just speak the words and it will be so". This man recognized his need, and who could help him. He didn't need to go to the local tabernacle. He called upon the Healer right where he was—where his need was greatest. Healing came with a spoken word or a touch. The woman in John 4 found forgiveness at a well. The thief hanging on a cross found his healing in the last moments of his life. The common denominator for all was not the *place* they went to, but the *One* they went to. The tax collector, the fisherman, the leper, the weak, the lost—all found their healing in one person—Jesus. It didn't matter what the location—on a mountainside, on the road to Jerusalem, in a house, in the temple. Where there was a need, God provided the healing.

Bring your broken and heavy-laden to His feet. Let your tears flow and let your heart be cleansed of guilt and shame. Call upon His sweet spirit to invest your soul with His holiness. Let the balm of Gilead flow over you and through you. Let Him bind your wounds and restore you. Set aside the world and all that encumbers you. Lonely and brokenhearted? Come, be healed. Guilt-ridden and ashamed? Come and be healed. Downtrodden and hopeless? Come.

Filled with doubt and fear? Come. Want to stand new and whole with the saints of all time? Come. Wherever you are...whatever your circumstance—Come. Come to Jesus and let Him enfold you in His holy embrace. Let His holy healing fill you. Let Jesus invest you with His holy spirit and make you His House of Holy Healing.

"But above all things, my brethren, swear not, neither by heaven, neither by the earth, neither by any other oath: but let your yea be yea; and your nay, nay; lest ye fall into condemnation."
~ James 5:12 ~

Meditation 25:

PROMISES

The sun was shooting beams of sunlight through the room. The warm breeze beckoned her outside and she felt like the new lambs, needing to just run and frolic in the grass. No matter she was a young woman now, soon to be married off and have a home of her own. The drudgery of daily chores wore on her spirit. She dare not ask her mother again to be released to the outdoors—the girl was wearing on her mother's last nerve with her pleading. But once she had caught glimpse of him coming over the rise, her mother could not keep the girl inside any longer. She was the only child and her father doted on her. Her father had been away for some time, and this daughter was excited to see him come home again. Looking just like a gazelle running through the field, the girl couldn't wait to jump into her father's outstretched arms. She wanted to take in all the smells of their reunion—the smell of sun and grass on his clothes, the feel of his whiskered face touching her cheek. She had dreamed of this reunion for so long. And now, it was about to happen. This will be a day of grand celebration. At the sight of his sweet daughter, the man fell to his knees, with his face in his hands, crying. As the girl approached her father, she could see the grief-stricken look upon his face. Was he injured from the battles he had encountered with the enemy?.... Was he ill from some disease?.... Was he weary from his long journey?.... Kneeling next to her father, the girl stroked his head and asked, "Father, are you not glad to see me?" To which the man cried, "Oh! My daughter! You have made me miserable and wretched, because I have made a vow to the Lord that I cannot break..." In despair, the man explained, "I made a vow to the Lord, saying 'if you give the Ammonites into my hands, whatever comes out of my house to meet me when I return in triumph from the Ammonites, will be the Lord's, and I will sacrifice it as a burnt offering...'" The girl rolled over from her knees to sit on the grass beside her beloved father. Looking off to the horizon, she sat in silence for only a brief time. Then, speaking in a voice too calm and mature for a girl of her few years, she replied...."My father, you have given your word to the Lord... do to me just as you promised now that the Lord has avenged you of your enemies..." After the girl completed her allotted time of love and farewell to her family and friends, the father did to her as he had vowed.... (Judges 11:30-39)

A vow was made... a vow was kept. Believing in the mercy and love of God—believing in the promises written in the Book for Living Eternally, Jephthah made a deal with God—"ok, God, I will do this if you do that". The contract was made. God did His part. And when the time came, Jephthah did his. And, so did his daughter. Look at the story once again. The girl didn't wail and bawl. She quietly honored her father's promise. She was raised to love and respect her father—and to trust him. She knew the cost to her—and to her father, yet she boldly stood up and took what was hers to do for honoring both her earthly father and her Heavenly father. The girl knew the value in giving one's word on a matter. This story of a father and daughter stands as testimony of the seriousness of making and keeping vows. Cry over the cost of his vow? *Absolutely.* Waiver in fulfilling his vow? N*ot once.* Deny God what was promised? *Never.* Trust that one day God would reward him for such faithfulness? *Forever.* I like to believe Jephthah and his daughter were rewarded for their faithfulness by being reunited to forever run through the fields of heaven.

The general definition of a "vow' is a solemn promise made before God or to God. Man is so flippant with his promises while God takes each one seriously. Man says with no thought, "I promise...". Remember when you were young and digging into mom's geraniums for fishing bait When scolded, you promised, "Mom, I won't do it again—*I promise*"—only to turn around and do it again. Or, remember when you forgot your books at school on purpose because you had something better to do than homework... "Honest, Dad, I won't forget again—*I promise*". What about the history test you conveniently forgot to study for after that. Or, remember the promise on the way home from work—*"I promise* I will not get caught up in that hurtful gossip clutch again". And the next day, in the break room, you were right back in the middle of it. What about the marriage vow to honor, love and respect one another *til death do you part...*? What about the promise made to the child to set aside personal desires to help him grow into a productive, respectful adult? What about the promise made in the Sunday school room to love Jesus and always keep him in the center? Or, the promises made each time we sing, "all to Jesus I surrender".... Did we?........ Do we?.........

When our word is given in a vow, an oath, a promise—can the receiver of that promise count on it to be fulfilled? The next time you say, *"I'll be there"*—make sure to you are. The next time you say, *"I will take care of it"*—do it. The next time you give your word—*keep it*. The next time you are ready to write off a promise made because it doesn't ft into your schedule of events or doesn't fulfill your current desires, take a minute to remember—remember God's promises to you. *"I will never leave thee, nor forsake thee."* (Hebrews 13:5) *"Verily, verily, I say unto you, He that believeth on me hath everlasting life."* (John 6:47) *"Lo, I am with you always, even unto the end of the world."* (Matthew 28:20) God promised Abraham a son—a son was delivered. God promised Noah the rain would come—the flood proves it. God promised deliverance for the captives—the sea split and the captives walked on dry land to their freedom. God promised David his seed would forever sit on the throne—Jesus, the root of David, sits at the right hand of our *King* for eternity. God promised a messiah, a deliverer—Jesus came. God promised the perfect sacrificial Lamb—on the cross, Jesus provided that. God promised to conquer death—the tomb proves it. God promised a comforter—the Holy Spirit came. There is no such thing as a casual promise to God. When God gives His word, you can take it to the bank. Can that be said of us?

Before you sing "...all to Jesus I surrender", make sure you are ready to do exactly that. Before you promise to stand for what is right and good and holy, no matter what comes, be sure you can follow through. Before you promise God to give all your heart to Him, be sure you haven't reserved a small piece away for yourself. Each time, before you utter, "I promise...", remember God's promises to you—and the cost of those promises He made. Each time before you disregard your oath, remember Jesus and the cost for Him to keep His promise. And, each time you are ready to say, "*I promise...*", remember Jephthah and his daughter.

"Trust in the LORD with all thine heart;
and lean not unto thine own understanding."
~ Proverbs 3:5 ~

Meditation 26:

LIVING BY FAITH

Many times as I have faced frightening situations, I am brought back to a song called "Living by Faith". As my mind runs through the words, there is a balm that soothes my suffering soul. As I would slip into the oblivion of sleep, these words would hold me fast to what was real and true... reminding me of who holds my life. As my heart agonizes over disappointment and hurt, He whispers, "Peace, be still". Facing the unknown, I put my faith in the One who created me and knows the plan He has for my life. He will not let me fall into dangerous waters that He doesn't throw a safety net around me. But, what does living by faith involve... how do we get to that place of sweet rest?

It's surrendering our will to the will of Almighty God. It's surrendering what *I* want to what "*He* wants"... "Father, not my will, but yours..." It's knowing our Heavenly Father on such an intimate level that we have no doubts of His great love and care for us. It's knowing the scriptures, not just in the mind, but *knowing* them in our hearts. It's imitating the life of Jesus, the Christ and Lord, who had no other desire but to be about His Father's business. Living by faith is... living in submission... living in confidence... living in content-ment... living in hope... living in trust... living in peace. Believing that whether in the storm or in the sunshine, in the valley or on the mountain, in a prison or a palace... our Lord will sustain us and see us through to receive the crown of life.

Not so long ago I heard a comment... silly wee comment I thought... "If you want to make God laugh, just tell Him *your* plans for your life..." "That's almost desecration toward my Lord!", I thought... "making jokes of my relationship with my Creator!" Then, as I mulled it around a bit more, I could see great truth in the statement. Man, in his own great importance takes his life in his own hands thinking he knows best what is good and right.... only to drop it, fracture it, pollute it. Then, with head bowed low, man takes the broken pieces of his life and gives them back to God to purify, re-shape and mold to His likeness again. (Or—at least the *wise* man does this.) Man in his own strength and power tries to outrun the angel of death only to find himself lying on his deathbed crying toward the heavens for a merciful God to rescue him from a dark eternity. Man in all his wisdom sacrifices all that is important and precious, stepping on friends and neglecting family to grab the riches of life only to sit alone in his big house, or big office, or big car, with his big bankbook as a pillow to weep upon as he longs for his Forever-Friend to comfort him. Giving up one's rights is only to gain the eternal right to sit with the Father and Son in Heaven. Giving up one's right to self-indulgence is to gain the privilege to become a servant sending the sweet aroma of self-sacrifice into the nostril of God. Giving up one's self-direction is to gain the comfort and joy that comes through faith that no matter the situation, God will work it for good for those that believe in Him.

Reading through an article called, "Daily Word", it spoke of "knowing that we are in the will of God brings much more comfort and joy than we could anticipate at the onset. God doesn't ask that much of us, but one thing He does ask is that we live our lives in obedience to Him. It most certainly is not easy to surrender total control of one's life to God. We tend to give God a portion and hold on to much more. We want control, we want to discover our own destiny. Eventually we find that our heart's desire was within the walls of God's plan that we had attempted so desperately to escape. Our hopes and our dreams live with God's plan. In committing our lives to God we can be assured that they are in capable hands. It is a waste of our time seeking after anything other than what God has intended for us. There are no promotions greater, and no material wealth of such value, that it can replace the perfect peace and contentment that our souls discover in God's perfect will. Whatever it may be. [taken from *"Daily Word"* - 02-17-04]

Tonight, before you lay your head on the pillow, ask your Heavenly Father to grant unto you (and the rest of the faithful remnant) the faith to go through the days ahead as our forefathers did. They walked in obedience and trust. They went about doing the tasks laid out before them confident that God would equip them for whatever waited down the road... sustain them through the tribulations... and rejoice with them at every victory. Knees still quake at the unknown, but they will not cave in. Hearts will suffer pain, but will not break. Lives will pause, but will not quit. Living by faith means trusting completely in One greater than ourselves. Living by faith means having confidence—*unshakable* confidence that no matter the circumstance, God will work it for good for those who love Him. So, come what may for us... we will commit to always do our best to be... *"Living by faith... in Jesus above... trusting, confiding in His great love..."*

"For we are but of yesterday, and know nothing,
because our days upon earth are a shadow"
~ Job 8:9 ~

Meditation 27:

SHADOWS

One day while driving along the countryside, I spotted a tree sitting alone in the middle of a grassy field. The late afternoon sun was casting a long shadow of the tree across the field. It caused me to remember the long shadow my dad's slim figure cast. At least, it seemed tall to a young girl. Then, as minds do sometimes, my mind began to wander and ponder along the subject of shadows. My dad was always a hardworking man, a man of honesty and loyalty, a man of his word. The shadow he cast was one of protection and integrity. In the last years of his life, this man cast a shadow of influence for righteousness and holiness, and a love for God's people. This journey down memory lane brought me to ponder what kind of shadow I might cast. Do I stand tall in honesty and loyalty? Is there protection and integrity within the lines of my shadow? Do I influence others in holiness? After I am gone, will others be touched by my shadow and remember fondly what was good and right about me?

In the book of Acts, in chapter 5, great fear seized the church because of persecution. Yet the apostles continued to preach the good news of the risen Christ. More and more men and women believed in the Lord and were added to the community of believers. As a result of the miracles the apostles were performing, and the Word spreading, people came and lined the streets hoping to get a glimpse of these extraordinary men—and to hear for themselves this amazing story. Their desire to believe was so strong that even the sound of the apostles' voices—even to be in the shadow they cast was enough for some. Am I living in such a way that others could be touched so traumatically for Christ by just the shadow of my life passing by?

Jonah was called by God to be His messenger to a lost and dying people in the village of Ninevah. Jonah, thinking himself wiser than God, set out in his own direction. As the story goes on, Jonah spent three days in the belly of the great fish to ponder his disobedience, and when Jonah was delivered from the fish's belly, there was a promise on his lips to always obey God. Yet, once again there was Jonah sitting in a desolate field in Ninevah, baking in the sun, suffering from his disobedience. And, once again God delivered Jonah by bringing a shadow of protection to cover this rebellious child so as not to lose him. How often do I cause God to rescue me from baking in my own disobedience?

There is comfort and protection for us in the shadow of our Heavenly Father. Scripture records God calling His children unto Him as a shepherd calls his sheep into the protection of the fold. From the beginning of time, the shadow of the cross hung over one of the Godhead. It wasn't a shadow of fear or shame. It was the shadow of love and obedience—the shadow of deliverance for the creation so loved by its Creator. In the midst of our guilt and sinfulness, we run to the cross and hide in the protection of its shadow. From the book of Genesis all the way through Revelation God has been calling us to come unto Him and live in His likeness, to live in such a way as to cast His shadow of holiness around about us.

So, once again I ask what kind of shadow am I casting. Is it a shadow that speaks of darkness and gloom? Or, is it a shadow that radiates the Light of an Almighty God who will spare not even His own beloved Son to bring about the safekeeping of my eternal soul? Is it a shadow of fear—or, a shadow that offers inner peace? What will the legacy that I leave behind be? Will they speak of the few good things I was able to accomplish? Will they remember that no matter the circumstance, my eyes were fixed on my Lord and Savior, and I lived out my life in the shadow of the cross—in the holiness of the cross? I pray that they will say she lived faithfully in the shadow of God's love.

*"Then sang Moses and the children of Israel this song unto the LORD, and spake, saying, I will sing unto the LORD, for he hath triumphed gloriously:
the horse and his rider hath he thrown into the sea. The LORD is my strength and song, and he is become my salvation: he is my God..."*
~ Exodus 12:1-2 ~

Meditation 28:

SONG ON MY HEART

The first song ever documented is introduced in Exodus 15. It is the song of deliverance Moses and the Israelites offered up after they had safely crossed the Red Sea. The song is an expression of gratitude and adoration, and a celebration of God's holiness, power and grace. "…The Lord is my strength and my song…He is my God, and I will praise Him…" (Ex. 15:2) It's not clear if instruments were used other than their voices. But we do know with certainty that this first verifiable song in history was a gospel song. Look at the last line: "..The Lord will reign forever and ever". (Ex. 15:18) With that in mind, it is easy to understand why mankind is drawn to the music that connects us with the very source of song. That connection is clearly the purpose for which music was created. [Paraphrased from an article in *Homecoming* magazine, July/August-2008 edition]

Music can transform a bleak countenance into one of joy and thanksgiving. A song is just made up of thought set to music—wee bits of theology to hum across the mind and heart.. And, when sung at the right moment, the song can create an ocean of emotion. Songs are expressions of feelings—loneliness, sorrow, fear, love, praise, hope, victory. Music can take the soul to that sweet place of communion with the Source. Music can transport a soul from its encumbered life to a secret place where no one else can enter—an oasis for rest and renewal.

John Newton found peace for his ravaged soul while he penned our beloved song, "Amazing Grace". Long hours spent on those slave-trading ships, how could he not be affected by the moans and cries of the captives held below deck. There was no place to go to get away from it. There was nothing but the sounds of the crew and the sea—and the misery. Convicted in his heart that this was a treacherous sin against God and mankind, John Newton needed a release. Unaware of the impact of his effort, he poured his heart out on paper and set it to music. Ever since, troubled souls have found their own release from guilt and shame in this song. "Amazing grace; how sweet the sound; that saved a wretch like me; I once was lost, but now am found; was blind, but now I see..." One man's folly? *Not hardly*. An expression of redemption? *Absolutely*. In the Library of Congress sits a registration for this song. It states that the words were written by John Newton; the melody by "Unknown". Well, you make your own conclusion, but for me—I believe the melody that came into John Newton's ear on that slave ship was directly from the heart of God to the hearts of those captives to the heart of a sinner saved by grace. "Unknown"? I want to meet Mr. Unknown when I get to heaven.

So often music has been a form of meditation for me—a garden of sweet communion. The melody is a balm for my twittered mind; the words, a message of healing. When loneliness surrounds me, the song, *"What a Friend We Have in Jesus"* reminds me of my true and faithful friend. "Never will I leave you nor forsake you", He promises. Jesus is with me always and forever. When my failures beat me down, my soul hears *"..His grace reaches me, yes, His grace reaches me, and twill last through eternity..."* When weariness overtakes me, I hear *"burdens are lifted at Calvary..."* When tears fill my soul, I hear *"God will wipe away all tears..."* When doubts knock at my heart's door, I hear *"living by faith in Jesus above, trusting, confiding in His great love..."* As fears grip my mind, my heart echoes, *"Because He lives, I can face tomorrow, because He lives all fear is gone; because I know He holds tomorrow, and life is worth the living just because He lives..."* When I wonder how my Lord could love me, I hear, *"When He was on the cross, I was on His mind..."* And when anxiety sets in at the thought of the death angel coming, I am reminded that *"When the darkness I see, He will be waiting for me; I won't have to cross Jordan alone..."* There is a song called *"Lord, Feed Your Children"*. The *Source* of music does that for me through the melodies He created. Music ministers to me in every way. It is a well of living water for my thirsty soul, manna for my hungry heart.

While in exile on the island of Patmos, apostle John had a vision. At one point in his vision, he witnessed every creature in heaven and on earth, and on the sea singing. What were they singing? *"To Him Who sits on the throne and to the Lamb be praise and honor and glory and power forever and ever."* (Revelation. 5:13) It was a song of worship and proclamation. The psalm writer speaks of singing a new song. He invites heaven and earth to join him in praise and worship to an awesome God. Why should we not lift our voices in song, whether in private or community worship to the God of our salvation? Why should we not find solace in music as it lifts us from our lowly struggles? For such is part of the fiber that makes up heaven—all things good and perfect.

I like to believe that music is a gift from God to offer us a mind's eye-view of our eternal home. The one thing that sticks in my mind when I recall author Don Piper's book, "90-Minutes in Heaven"—is his account of the beautiful music he heard. The amazing singing, the voices all in one accord. Picture it! And let your mind hear the perfect music. Angels and all the heavenly host singing praises to God. And there was Don—right in the middle of it all. That's where I long to be. All the voices in perfect pitch and harmony, and me right in the middle of that heavenly choir, my voice on key and in rhythm. *"Then sings my soul, my savior God to thee; how great thou art...."* This is one concert I do not want to miss!

Blessed is he that readeth, and they that hear the words of this prophecy, and keep those things which are written therein...
~ Revelation 1:3 ~

FUZZY RECEPTION

It was a normal workday. The keys on my computer were clicking away, the printer was running smooth, the birds were chirping outside the office window, and the radio was blasting away on a local Christian station. Everything seemed clear and crisp in my world. Oops! There was a faint buzz to the radio reception. It passed almost before I noticed, but it did intrude upon my oasis—and the song that was playing. A few minutes later, there it was again, only a bit longer this time. Not more than a couple minutes later, it came full force – static interference with the radio reception. Before long, the station I was listening to was completely lost to the static noise and I couldn't make out a single word. I stopped my work, got up and went over to the radio to try to tune that station back. There it was. The songs were coming through with clarity and sharp reception. The good stuff was filling my ear once again and the fuzzy noise was gone.

Is there a lesson in that radio experience? It caused me to think of how many times I let the world cause static between me and the Holy Spirit, blocking a clear reception. With the radio, all it takes sometimes is an innocent airplane passing over to break the signal. Sometimes all it takes is a stubbed toe or a missed parking spot to break the holy signal and let the garbage back in. There are complex devices available to super charge the reception for radios. There are devices to increase the power of the computer signal, sending it around the world. There are even devices to help the signals from the brain to reach the appropriate damaged nerve centers, or devices to help the signal to the heart. What kind of devices are there to increase the signals for the soul? What can we do to increase the strength of our antenna and make sure the message from our Holy Spirit comes through uninterrupted?

Ever been in a car traveling down the road, jamming to a radio station, and just as your favorite song comes on, you start to lose reception? Before long, you are so far down the road you can't find the radio station at all. So often I have found myself in tune with the Holy Spirit and traveling down the path of righteousness. Or, at least that was what I thought. Things start going wrong. The days are hard, the burdens seem to pile up, and I feel the weight of the world. It's somewhere in the midst of this heap that I realize I had gotten so far down the wrong road I couldn't hear the Holy Spirit any longer. I had lost reception. I hadn't prayed before heading out to start the day. I had ignored a fellow pilgrim who was in need of help. I had set aside my daily Bible reading and meditation because I had deadlines to meet and family matters to tend to. At this point I must stop everything, get up and go tune in the Holy Spirit again. It's important to spend time in God's word, reading and studying, filling those brain waves with holy information. It's equally important to spend time in quiet meditation and communion with God, reflecting on His goodness.

Thick fog and storms obscure the view for the airplane pilot and cause him to depend solely on the radar in his ship to guide the ship to safety. If something interferes with that radar signal, the plane is lost. There are times in each life when the Christian can't see clearly, and has only God's holy radar for guidance. It's during those times the Christian must trust God to bring him through the storm. For this Christian, personally, I know that it has been in the midst of those storms in my life, I have felt closest to God because I am so totally dependent upon Him. He is at the forefront of my thoughts, my prayers, my dreams. So often I would plead with God to remove the storm, to take it away. Only when I fall to my knees and give all to Him do I hear His beam of guidance come through. When I sit in the hush of my collapse and hopelessness, I hear Him whisper

"I won't take it away, but I will bring you through it". The signal is restored and I feel my "ship" being guided to safety—safety in His promises that the overcomer will come through to wear a crown and spend eternity with Him.

Satan sends out a strong signal too. We must not forget that. His demons of wickedness are permeating everything taken in through the eyes and ears. Satan sends signals to the brain speaking thoughts of discontent, jealousy, pride, ego, greed, lust, immorality, dishonesty. He is the father of lies and everything evil. Satan has one mission alone—to seek and destroy. Satan roams to and fro over the earth seeking an opportunity to destroy a soul. He is a sleeked source of wickedness coming in subtly at first. Satan's signal beams in interfering with the holy signal. Messages come softly like, "you deserved that job over your co-worker", or, "just a quick look at those x-rated pictures wouldn't hurt anything", or, "you don't need the responsibility of a family right now. Just get rid of it", or the infamous "surely you won't die from one little taste". The snare is set, the soul steps in, and finds himself trapped in the pit of destruction. The soul is doomed to that pit of darkness for eternity unless he makes a move to change the reception and tune in the beam of holiness. Satan's signal is strong. But praise God! God's signal is stronger. God can override Satan's signal if we have an ear to hear. God offers a message of forgiveness, mercy, redemption, and hope. God's signal guides the soul on the holy path of righteousness—the path that leads to an eternal home in Heaven where all is set right.

Lessons from a fuzzy radio signal. Well, maybe it's far-fetched and stretching a bit. But it caused this Christian to sit up and take notice, to ponder the signals I am allowing into my "receptor'. The most profound lesson that hit me from this is that I need to stay in tune with God. It is vital to my soul that I am constantly fine-tuning in order to increase the signal the Holy Spirit is offering. And the best device available to me is the Bible lying on my desk. I must pick it up daily and spend time reading those precious bits of scripture handed down so carefully over the centuries. I must seek God every day, in the beginning, middle and end of the day. He is ever with me if I will just tune Him in. Let the words from Albert Brumley's popular song leave the final impression.

"Come and listen in to a radio station, where the mighty host of Heaven sing...If you want to hear the songs of Zion, coming from the land of endless spring, Get in touch with God...Turn your radio on...And listen to the music in the air, ...and glory to share...Turn the lights down low...And listen to the Master's Radio, get in touch with God ....Turn your radio on."

Greater love hath no man than this,
that a man lay down his life for his friends.
~ John 15:13 ~

Meditation 30:

I LOVE YOU TO DEATH

Once there was a silly movie that brought the viewer—me—to become a puddle of mush as I watched it. The story was about the unlikely relationship of a young woman and a giant gorilla named "Joe". Maybe you know the movie, "Mighty Joe". Joe trusted the woman to seek only good for him as he did for her. The woman came to trust people of the world to help her protect Joe. But it wasn't long before the woman discovered that these new friends had only one thing in mind—exploit the gorilla for their own gain. Toward the end of the movie came the part that reduced me to a puddle of tears. The giant gorilla is on the run from authorities trying to escape to a place that feels safe and familiar to him. The authorities see the gorilla as a menace on the loose and want him destroyed. They don't understand him, nor does he understand them. Joe is scared and alone. While searching for his friend (the young woman), Joe finds himself in an amusement park, drawn there by the spotlight. In the midst of the din, Joe hears that familiar voice calling to him. At the same time Joe also hears the cries of a little boy. The boy is in a dangerous situation. The giant gorilla recognizes that he is the only one capable of saving the child. To save the boy would mean danger for Joe, captivity and probably death. Turning first to his friend who offers familiarity and safety, and then to the child whose life is in danger, Joe makes the choice to do the only thing he could do—ignore his own safety and rescue the little boy. Mighty Joe takes off to the top of the burning structure to reach the boy just in time—only to fall to the ground with an earth-shaking thud. As the giant gorilla lies there lifeless, the small boy rests safe and secure in the palm of Joe's mighty hand. The child was handed off to his mother, the young woman cries softly over her long-time friend. (This is where I started weeping aloud.) "Don't leave me", she whispers through her tears. The onlookers stood silent now—all those who wanted the gorilla dead were there with mouths gaping at the astounding feat of self-sacrifice they had just witnessed. True to movie endings, the gorilla ended up only stunned by the fall. Everyone cheered as the gorilla touches the cheek of his companion. Because of the great generosity of some kind-hearted souls, Mighty Joe and the young woman return to their jungle home where the gorilla would be free to roam in a game reserve supervised by his friend. They were home again to live happily ever after. As the movie ended I wiped my tears and chastised myself for getting so emotional over a movie about a fictitious gorilla. Then I started seeing some spiritual truths within the story.

In the Bible, in the book of John, chapter 13, Jesus asks the question, "Will you lay down your life for me?" Jesus knew the answer before Peter gave it. He knew that Peter, with all his good intentions, would deny the very one he was now proclaiming his undying allegiance to. Have you ever professed unbounded service to Christ and then found yourself in a situation where you had to make a choice—take an unpopular stand for righteousness, or cling to the safety of the crowd and go along with the flow even though it was wrong. Me too! The scoffers and mockers stood silent at the foot of the cross as the earth shook and the sun refused to shine. The ones who sought to destroy Jesus were the very ones He went to the cross to save. Jesus asks us to lay down our lives that we might enjoy eternal life with Him. It is when I truly give up everything—lose everything, then I can gain everything. If only we could get a grip on that concept, what a blessed life of peace we would enjoy, and rich fulfillment.

Someone named Fenelon made a statement that goes, "Peace of heart lies in the perfect resignation to the will of God. Put all things in His hands, and offer them beforehand to Him in your hearts, as a sacrifice." A girl named Rachel Scott found herself in such a situation where she was forced to demonstrate her "peace of heart". It was an ordinary day at school. She had good friends and a loving family, and she had plans for her future—a future that had God at the center. Rachel didn't hide her commitment to God. And on this day she was faced with a choice—deny Christ to save her life, or proclaim Him as Lord of her life and die. The assailant asked Rachel, "Do you believe in Jesus?" Rachel looked down the barrel of his gun, then into his eyes, and answered firmly, "Yes." One minute the young teen was making plans. The next, she was looking into the face of a crazed gunman. And, then, she was looking into the face of Jesus as He welcomed her home. Rachel Scott understood John 13:38. She understood self-denial and perfect peace of heart. In her short years on earth, Rachel Scott understood that serving Jesus Christ meant more than pew-sitting, potluck supper, or a dribble in the contribution plate. She had made a willful choice to give her life to her Lord and Savior, no matter the cost. And, that's exactly what this child of God did.

Back to Joe, the gorilla. Experience had taught him that humans meant danger. Yet one small human needed help, and Joe was the only one who could supply what the child needed. Setting his fears aside, ignoring the opportunity to escape, Joe embraced the ones who wanted to destroy him. He laid down his very life for another. Jesus Christ did that very thing for sinful man—for sin-filled me. Author, Max Lacado, puts it this way, "Never did the obscene come so close to the holy as it did on Calvary. Never did the good in the world so tightly intertwine with the bad as it did on the cross. Never did the right involve itself so intimately with wrong as it did when Jesus was suspended between Heaven and earth." (taken from "No Wonder They Call Him Savior", by Max Lacado) God's people have been called to be messengers to the lost, to walk as pathways of Light to the dark world. How can we refuse to lay down our lives to a holy God who loves us so desperately that even before creation, He set in motion the plan for redemption to bring us back to Him. Convicted of such a truth, I must examine my heart for any thread of self-serving thoughts that might linger there. I must ask God to remove those threads. Only then can I live in perfect peace as I offer up my life to Jesus, my Lord and Master—who set the example.

After that movie about Mighty Joe, and after recalling the story of Rachel Scott, I pleaded with God to bless me with that spirit of self-sacrifice and strong faith demonstrated in these. I want to imitate Jesus in His love for the Father—and me.

This is the day which the LORD hath made;
we will rejoice and be glad in it.
~Psalm 118:24~

HEY DUDE...WATCH YOUR ATTITUDE

A man was passing by a tattoo parlor where the owner was outside sweeping his walkway. The passer-by caught glimpse of an advertisement for a tattoo. It read "Born Loser". The passer-by commented absentmindedly, "who would ever want that tattoo on his body". The old proprietor replied in broken English, "Before tattoo on body, must first tattoo on mind".

Researchers, psychologists, scholars, and Dr. Phil have all told us how the attitude of the mind forms the person. If a man lives with an attitude of defeat, he most certainly will not succeed. On the other hand, the man who lives with the attitude that he can accomplish anything he sets his mind to do—this man will most certainly achieve great things. All agree that when man believes in his mind that he is a loser, then he will live as a loser.

One Sunday some years ago, I was feeling especially burdened with the struggles of life.

Slipping away from the assembly gathered in a routine fellowship meal, and seeking a quiet place to meet with God, (and yes, sulk a bit), I retreated to the stillness of our empty auditorium where the saints gathered to worship. Without turning the lights on, I sat down on a pew to bask in the warmth the room offered. The sun was filtering in through the stained-glass windows, wrapping me in rainbows of color. It was going to be my garden to meet with my Heavenly Father. As I sat quite content in my solitude and meditation and humming a familiar hymn to myself, my sanctuary was invaded by someone bursting through the door. Still as a statue, I tried to not be disturbed from my quiet place, still humming. Maybe the intruder would get the idea that I wanted to be alone. Oh no, here he comes. Mercy! Can't a person just be left alone! Then it came. "What cha doin'?", asked the young boy. My brain was screaming, "Go away! Can't you see that I want to be alone with God to unload my burdens". But, instead of beating my young intruder with a verbal stick, I politely replied that I was just sitting and singing. "I'll sing with you", he volunteered. Humor him and he will go away, I thought. So, for the next few minutes, my unwanted companion and I sang together, mostly songs of his choosing. "Number 17", he said. "Hallelujah, Praise Jehovah". Oh my! This song was hard for even the best singers, but we forged ahead. He sang out with gusto, and I just sort of joined in, both of us croaking like frogs rather than singing like the angels. "Let's sing 155—it's my mom's favorite" he continued. We were quite the unlikely duo. And, so we went along for a few more minutes before others started to come in for the next worship service. My singing buddy left me to join his family, and I was preparing myself for service. It was then that I realized my countenance had changed. I had gone in sullen and down and wanted to meet with God alone so He would uplift me. God came to me in the form of a wee boy, bespectacled in innocence and faith. In spite of his mere 11 years, he had ministered to my sagging soul in a way no one else could at that point in time. God did not allow me what I wanted—to stay in my private pity party. He sent me what I needed—someone to cause me to let go of my self-serving attitude and enjoy the blessings around me. I needed an attitude adjustment, and God sent me just that.

There is a poem that tells that if a child grows up with criticism, he learns to criticize. It's true. If a child grows up in hate, he learns to hate. If a child grows up around defeated people, he will be defeated himself. If a child is told he is worthless and never to amount to anything, he will grow to be useless to everyone, including himself, never trying to achieve a thing. If the child grows up with wickedness and evil around him, he will surely be wicked and evil. If an adult starts out thinking he won't make it to the finish of whatever he is doing, he will surely not see it completed. On the other hand, if a child grows up with love, he will love others. If a child grows up with praise and respect, he will pass it along. If the child grows up with God at the center of his family, he will walk with God all his life. If the adult says to himself, "I can do this", he will accomplish all things he puts his hand to. That's the attitude to carry. Shake off the negative, destroying attitude and hold tight to the attitude that tells us we can do all things through Christ who gives us strength.

What kind of song best describes the attitude you started out this day with? "Make The World Go Away"... "Raindrops Keep Falling On My Head'... "I'll Do It My Way"... "I'm Mister Lonely".... "Don't Worry, Be Happy"... "Oh, What A Beautiful Morning"... "I've Got Joy, Joy, Joy Down In My Heart"......... The psalmist talks about singing a new song—*"Sing to the Lord all the earth, sing to the Lord, praise His name, proclaim His salvation day after day... sing to the Lord a new song, for He has done marvelous things..."* (Psalm 96:1-2, 98:1) He had an attitude of praise and thanksgiving. In Philippians 2, we are told to have the same attitude (mind) as Christ. And what was that, one might ask. Christ made Himself nothing, taking the very nature of a servant, humbled Himself, and became obedient even to death on a cross. This section also instructs that we should do everything without complaining or arguing, so that we may become blameless and pure–children of God without fault. Can you picture Jesus having a bad attitude? "I don't want to teach today. It's hot and I want to go for a boat ride." "I'm tired, so I'm going to sleep in today because I deserve a rest." Of course they should wait on me—I'm the Son of God after all." "Tell that hungry rabble to go feed themselves—I have a headache." "Go away—I need time for myself." Good Grief! The Son of God would never think like that! A child of God would never be so self absorbed! So—why are *we*?

Now this isn't to say there is not a time that the weary Christian must steal away for some private time for renewal and refreshing of the body and spirit. Jesus did that. He slept in a boat, He rested on a hilltop, He sat by a well. But, He never turned away from a soul in need of Him. He never had a mindset of anything but service and love. Greed, selfishness, pride, laziness, lust, complaining, grumbling —these were never words describing the mindset of Christ. His was an attitude of grace, forgiveness, service, compassion and love. He took on the form of man to come to earth on a seek-and-rescue mission. There was no time for bad attitudes or downcast countenance. He was on a tight schedule, and there was much work that needed to be done. He left the glory of Heaven to come down to set an example of excellence for man to follow. So, it's no wonder the scripture writer was inspired by the Holy Spirit to pen, *"Let this mind (attitude) be in you, which was also in Christ Jesus"*. (Philippians 2:5)

There are a lot of things in life we cannot change or control. The family we are born into, the actions of others, and the infamous fact of death and taxes. However, we can change and control our attitudes. We can sulk and pout because the day isn't going as we had hoped. Or, we can just make lemonade out of the lemons. In the Disney movie, *Pollyanna*, there is a game the little girl plays called the "glad game". The thrust of the game is to find something to be glad about in each and every situation. One example was when the girl was visiting with the house staff. The adults were complaining about the fact that it was Sunday, and that meant a fiery sermon full of shouting from a grim preacher, and extra work preparing a feast at lunchtime. When the cook grumbles, "What is there to be glad about in this day", Pollyanna replied, "We can be glad that it is seven whole days before Sunday comes again!" Get the idea? Well the whole town got the idea of the glad game, and it changed the beat of this small community. Equipped with an attitude of gladness and thanksgiving, the people were kinder to one another—even the preacher was softer in his delivery of glad tidings from the pulpit. A simple attitude adjustment made a huge difference in every life.

When the bad days come—and come they will, cry a little, reflect a little. But then seek out the blessing in the situation. Let the goodness and light of God shine through the darkness. Be like Pollyanna and play the glad game. Don't tattoo "loser" on your mind. Instead tattoo "winner" across your mind and life. Pay heed to the Holy Spirit when He nudges you and says, "Hey dude—you need a new attitude". Let the attitude of Christ live in you and through you.

"… and from Jesus Christ, who is the faithful witness, the firstborn from the dead, and the ruler of the kings of earth… To Him who loves us and has freed us from our sins by His blood…be power and glory forever and ever."
~ Revelation 1: 5 ~ [NIV]

FREEDOM

Freedom is something most of us have lived with for all of our lives. Sometimes I have wondered how it was that I was blessed to be born and live in a country that proclaims to be the "land of the free". Freedom of speech, freedom of work, freedom to vote, freedom to walk across the land without fear, freedom to education, freedom to have money and use it according to my choice, freedom of religion….. Freedom of religion…. I am free to worship whomever, however, wherever I see fit. But, am I? Am I really *free*?

The dictionary describes "freedom" as the absence of slavery; the ability to go and do as one desires. So, according to the dictionary I am free. Right? My physical being is not enslaved to a master who controls my comings and goings, my conversations. But, what about my spiritual being? Where does my spirit stand? Freedom or slavery?

Slavery was common in Biblical times. Many served others in bondage. The law of Moses provided for the "Year of Jubilee", when slaves were given the opportunity to gain their freedom. (Leviticus 25) The exodus of the people of Israel from Egypt is an example of God bringing His people out of slavery into freedom. Those people were released from physical bondage. (Exodus 7) But true, ever-lasting freedom for the soul came in the form of Jesus Christ. In Galatians 5, it tells us that the believer must "stand fast in the liberty in which Christ has made us free, and be not entangled again in the yoke of bondage..." "What yoke?", you may ask. "I am not bound by any yoke". Sin is the yoke that binds us to earth and away from our Holy Father. Sin enslaves; Christ sets free. Sin breaks families, breaks relationships, breaks character. Sin brings guilt and shame as its companions. Sin blackens hearts. Sin separates from God. Set free from sin by Christ Jesus, the believer enjoys an everlasting *year of jubilee.*

Jesus explained to His followers that when people know the truth, the truth will set them free. While enjoying the freedom to indulge in certain behaviors, certain lifestyles, certain thought patterns, the heart is bound all the same by the guilt and shame brought on by these actions. Out of this perverted nature arises sin. Sin is not just absence of good, or an unwise behavior that causes sorrow and distress. Sin is a rebellion against God's standard of righteousness—against God Himself. Sin has been defined as the "faithless rebellion of the creature against the just authority of his creator. Sin is actually a contradiction to the holiness of God, whose image we bear". Against the dark background of sin and its reality, the Gospel comes as the good news of deliverance that God has provided through His Son. Jesus bears the penalty of sin in place of His people. Jesus redeems us, looses us from the bondage of sin—the death sentence that sin holds over the soul Jesus pardoned by *His* death and resurrection. The blood of Jesus, Son of the living God, washes away the bleakness of sin and gives back hope—hope of a new life, and a promise for eternity. Romans 6 says that now that we have been set free from sin, and have become slaves to God, the benefit we reap leads to holiness, and the result is eternal life. It goes on to say the wages of sin is death, but the gift of God is eternal life in Christ Jesus, our Lord. By surrendering our self-will, our wicked ways and thoughts, our fears, and giving back to God our hearts, souls, and minds—only then do we know true freedom. There is a song by Christian artist, Ray Bolts, that causes me to think of what I have been given, the freedom I have by surrendering all to Christ. Ray Boltz writes, "I have made choices that I know weren't right... traded my tomorrow, and all I have to show for it is guilt and shame... (God) He took this life full of sorrow, and suddenly everything changed...it was like walking in the darkness when a light came shining through... God gave me back my tomorrow..."

Thank God, I have back my hope for tomorrow. Because of God's love—because of the sacrifice offered up in the form of the precious blood of Jesus, the beloved Son of God—I am free. I am an ordinary person, a sinner saved by grace. I live and breath in freedom—the freedom to give myself up for Christ's sake. It is when I surrender everything to Him, that I really gain everything. Hold tight to the blessed freedom found in the life lived totally committed to God. May God bless us to continue to enjoy waving the flag of freedom. May He bless us to treasure in our hearts the freedom bought at such a high price as the life of the Precious Lamb. May God bless us to forever proclaim, "Praise God, I am free at last!"

So teach us to number our days,
that we may apply our hearts unto wisdom.
~ Psalm 90:12 ~

Meditation 33:

BUCKET LIST

It was group time at the local children's home. The children come together according to their units along with their counselors to discuss various topics. This particular evening, the counselor was prompted by the latest hit movie, "Bucket List" to ask his group of boys to make their own "bucket list"—things they wanted to do before they died. As one might imagine from adolescent boys, the list covered the sports arena and exciting activities... "Ride in a air force jet"... "Meet Michael Jordan"... "Play pro football"... "Own a zoo"... "Kiss a girl'... Some items on the list took on a more serious tone giving a hint of the child's situation in life... "Be a part of a family"... "Be a better parent than mine were to me"... "Live with God at my side"... "Meet God when I die".....

What would your list include? My list of things to do before I die would include cleaning out my file cabinet, organize and label all my photos, reach my ideal weight and stick to it, and sample everything on the menu at Taco Bell. You might scold me and tell me to stop kidding, to which I would reply, "who's kidding". Those things just mentioned might be better itemized in a list titled "wishful thinking". The main thing I hope to accomplish before I die is to make a difference for the better in one person's life. My heart yearns to make life better for those I love and care about. Not better in terms of worldly possessions (although I would love to lavish on them their every desire), but *better* in terms of being equipped to successfully get through every circumstance in life. I want so desperately for them to know the riches wrapped up in a deep relationship with God.

There was a man in Jerusalem called Simeon. He was a devout and righteous man. It was revealed to him by the Holy Spirit that he would not die before he had seen the Christ. Every day he went to the temple to pray. On this particular day a young couple brought their male child to the temple to present him to the Lord as was the custom. Simeon saw the child, took him in his arms and praised God, saying, "*Sovereign Lord, as you have promised, you now dismiss your servant in peace. For my eyes have seen your salvation...*" (Luke 2:28-30) Simeon could depart in peace for his bucket list was complete. He had laid eyes upon the Promised One.

While the men in the movie had been given their death sentence from disease and illness, they weren't satisfied to sit around and just wait for it to happen. They made a plan, wrote a list, and set out to accomplish many things before their time was up. One by one they checked off the items on their lists. They recognized that their days were numbered and there was no time for procrastination. They were focused and determined. There is a story of a man and a jar of marbles. The man had a theory that went like this—he said:

"The average person lives about seventy-five years. Multiply 75 (average life span) times 52 (weeks in a year), which comes to 3900—which is the number of Saturdays the average person has in his entire lifetime. It took me until I was about 55 years old to think about this in detail, and by the time I had lived through over 2800 Saturdays. I got to thinking that if I lived to be 75, I only had about a thousand of them left to enjoy. So, I went to the store and bought every single marble they had. I ended up visiting 3 stores before I rounded up 1000 marbles. I took them home and put them inside a large, clear jar, and placed the jar where it was readily visible. Every Saturday since then, I have taken one marble out and thrown it away. I found that by watching the marbles diminish, I focus more on the really important things in life. There is nothing like watching your time on earth run out to help get your priorities straight."

It wasn't long before I got my own jar of marbles. The man had said to take one marble and throw it away—*away*, never to be added back to the heap. There are 1000 marbles in my jar—*only*

1000 marbles. Made me pause to think of how I was using my days on earth. I have a job that I give my days to. I have family who I give my time to. I am a Christian and give my time to the work of Christ. Someone once said that it's not enough just to have absence of sin in a life, but that life must be lived for righteousness as a testimony to others. I need to live my days as a walking, talking testimony to others so the marbles of my life have meaning. What I need to give testimony to is the tremendous inner peace my soul enjoys through a loving and reverent relationship with my Heavenly Father. I need to take my experiences with God and share them with others. I can only *imagine* what relief the adulterous woman felt when Jesus told her she was forgiven. But I can *tell* with conviction and credibility of the mercy and grace poured over me, and the great release my heart felt from my heavy burden of sin. I can tell of the blessed grace that flows over me continually. I can stand as a beacon of light in the darkness. I can listen with holy ears to hear the Shepherd's call above the din of the world. In my quest to make my marbles count for something, I have learned to make the most of the opportunities each day brings; to attempt to live righteous before God and men; to enjoy the ordinary, simple blessings in each day; to be watchful of the snares laid out for me by Satan; to stand ready to give an answer for the hope within me; and live in perfect peace with God.

One day my time on earth will be over, and I will be taken up to stand before the Judge of all time. I will feel a gentle hand reach for mine. I will look into the loving face of my Lord, and I will hear Him say, "She is one of ours, Father. She has served us well, and lived each day fully alive in our Spirit." Until then, my list of things to do before I die has only two items on it—live my life pleasing to God, and, take as many people as I can to Heaven with me. What is on your bucket list?

For since by man came death, by man came also the resurrection of the dead. For as in Adam all die, even so in Christ shall all be made alive.
~ 1 Corinthians 15:21-22 ~

A WALK IN THE GARDEN

Gardens. Spring brings the planning and planting of a garden. Summer brings the excitement of bounties emerging from the garden. Autumn brings harvest of produce from the garden. Winter brings longing and dreaming of the gardens that were, and the gardens to come. Some people gain their livelihood from their gardens. Farmers spend hours diligently studying over facts and figures from last year's crops, planning for the current year. Hobbyists spend hours dreaming about the shades and hues of all the colors that will adorn their gardens. Along with the dreaming and planning comes a responsibility to protect the fruits of their labor from the varmints who would also like to enjoy a munch here or there on what grows in the garden. A garden is the legitimate excuse for an adult to get dirty.

The thought of a garden can bring a more spiritual pattern to mind. Gardens are mentioned throughout the Bible, both literally and figuratively. Three specific gardens come to my mind. Once I heard a phrase tossed out which no one knew the source. It goes like this—"What one man lost in a garden, another gained in a garden." Of course, the gardens were Eden and Gethsemane.

Adam, the very first farmer, was placed by God in the midst of the Garden of Eden to work and tend it. (Genesis 2:15-ff) Adam was free to enjoy anything from the garden except from the Tree of Knowledge of Good and Evil. And Adam walked in peace and harmony with the Creator and creation. But it wasn't long before the serpent, more subtle than any of the rest, came along to change the atmosphere of the garden for Adam. Adam buckled to the temptation before him, blinded by the subtleties around him, deafened to the truth speaking to him from his heart. Thus, the curse was upon mankind and all of creation. What was once a relationship of total focus, trust, and obedience now held shadows of shame and guilt. The garden tranquility, unity, and peace of this garden was distorted by sin, and the blood of innocents would be required to atone for it.

Spanning over to another garden in Matthew 26, we see a young man on His knees. He is praying there alone. In the cool of the night this man named Jesus is pouring his heart out, sweating so much His sweat fell heavy like drops of blood. He was reaching out to the Father for strength for what lay ahead. Although we recognize the agony and loneliness that went into the garden that night, let us not forget the peace and obedience that came out of that garden. This was the garden where Jesus went to meet with His Father, His Master, His King and make the final commitment to fulfill the purpose for a member of the Godhead to come to earth. In this garden, Jesus accepted the burden of sin for all mankind. In this garden man's way back to the Creator was made clear.

The third garden I visited in my mind's journey was the garden near Golgotha's hill. In this garden there was a new tomb in which no one had ever been laid. It is here they laid the crucified body of Jesus. In this garden Mary Magdalene cried, first in grief over the loss of her beloved friend, and then in joy over the news from the "Gardner". Mary heard her name softly spoken in the garden. Not only did she hear her name, but Mary heard hope and security, promise and peace. In this garden prophecy was fulfilled, the path of redemption was laid, the price was paid in full. The soul of sinful man was bought back by the blood of the Lamb one time, for all time. The dead body of Jesus was carried into this garden and placed in the tomb. The resurrected body of Jesus, alive and well, walked out victorious, leaving behind the grave clothes that once bound Him. Death was defeated and the saints for all eternity were rejoicing.

The next time you hold a rose in your hand and get pricked by the rose's thorns, let that remind you of the subtleness of sin still around and in us. The next time you fight the hard ground to keep the this-tles from strangling your lush greens, remember the serpent is still alive and thriving, whispering deceit in any ear that will listen. The next time you are sitting in the cool of the evening, remember the innocent man sweating because of the task before Him. Whenever you stroll down a garden path, ask yourself if you are walking in peace and harmony with your Creator. With each step, with each breath, let us listen with our ears and our hearts to the words cried in a garden so long ago—*"Not my will, but Thine be done"*. As we enjoy the harvest of our garden, let us not be duped to believe that sin doesn't matter, that sin is not so serious. Let us remember the picture of the young man stepping from the garden in obedience and love, ready to fulfill God's plan for Him—the plan of redemption. Let us remember that image as we step up to the hoe and work our "garden' to bring about the fruit of His spirit.

Are they not all ministering spirits,
sent forth to minister for them who
shall be heirs of salvation?
~Hebrews 1:14 ~

Meditation 35:

ANGELS AMONG US

Scripture talks about ministering angels, and angels watching over God's people. Of course we know the Bible is written truth. But I also know this to be true from personal experience. Angels have ministered to me all through my life. It started the day I was born into a family of ministering angels, and has continued through the years, right up to this very moment.

The early years brought ministering angels in the form of friends, neighbors, physicians, and teachers. It was any ordinary neighborhood by sight, but look closer. Not so many neighbors would make sure the little crippled girl got to play neighborhood softball along with everyone else. Not every neighborhood would continually gather around one house to visit because the family couldn't leave their sick child to go elsewhere. Not every neighborhood of mothers would offer support with cookies and babysitting siblings while one mother had to make weekly trips to medical facilities with their sick daughter. Not every neighborhood had kids who would congregate in the same worn out yard day after day just so the crippled girl could be a part of their play. Not every neighborhood would surround one family with love and encouragement as their little girl struggled with constant pain and sickness. But ours did. Not every teacher would go the extra mile to help a child reach her potential mentally. Mine did. Not every physician would search every possible avenue for a better treatment, and spend most days consulting colleagues, articles, and journals for answers why a child should be experiencing such a debilitating disease. But mine did. Ministering angels, each one.

At the special school I attended, not all the kids had families who accepted and loved them. But mine did. Some children had parents who couldn't (or wouldn't) care for their special-needs child. But mine did. My parents worked so hard to give my brothers and me a good life. In the early years, my dad worked three jobs in an effort to stay ahead of the flood of medical bills — and even the ordinary bills. In his off time (which was rare), my dad always made time for his kids. Even though he suffered summer-time allergies, there he was mowing down the weeds covering the empty lot so the softball games could go on. He thrilled at each milestone we accomplished, and set us straight when we would waiver from the right. Dad made it a point to be home for supper every night to touch base with his young family. And, before heading off to another job, he would pat the boys on the head, and give me a push on the swing. As we grew, he would take my older brother along to work on his secondary jobs, or take my younger brother out to catch fishing bait. One of our family rituals in those days was to wait for our dad to call that it was time to come to the gas station and "help" him close shop. Off we would go, so excited to be with him wherever he was. Mom was no slouch through all this. She worked hard to keep our home a place of refuge for all of us. Because my illness took so much of her time, Mom didn't work outside our home. But she worked hard as a wife and mother. She set the mode for getting ready for dad to come home. Or, she would make picnics to take to where Dad was working so the family could share a meal together. Even though so much of her attention was focused on my illness, Mom never slighted her other children. Mom was there for her friends and neighbors all the while tending the needs, great and small, of her family. Dad would make toys for us — garages for the boys, and doll furniture for me. He was always making things to help his crippled daughter have a full life. Mom continually offered love and support to her family. At one point, my disease was so severe and pain so intense that I couldn't hardly move in the mornings. My dad would gently lift me from the bed to carry me to a warm bath my mom had prepared. There I would soak the pain away before we could start the day. Mom would sit for hours with me in doctors' offices. Both Mom and Dad would continue to encourage me through each hurtle, and praise me on each accomplishment. Ministering angels of love.

Siblings are supposed to fight and be jealous of one another. Not us. My two brothers doted on me—still do. As youngsters, my older brother would cart me around the neighborhood in our wagon. At the neighborhood ballgames, he made sure I got to play too. Mom would offer up her broom for my bat. Dad would pitch a grounder ball to me, and my brother would pick me up and run the bases each time my mighty broom made contact with the ball. Big sisters are supposed to look after their younger siblings. However, in our family, my younger brother looked after me. He played dolls with me (he always used his "GI Joe" doll), and let me choose the games. When we were older, he would always be home to carry me upstairs for bed. Once grown into adulthood, both brothers brought their babies and placed them in my arms to love and nurture as my own. And nowadays, those "babies" bring their babies to me. I just utter a need, and a host of family come to lovingly fulfill whatever it may be. Ministering angels each one.

All grandparents are required to spoil grandchildren. Mine were no exception. They were there offering cookies, milk, advice and love. Once I was spending the day with one grandma. She looked up from her ironing and made me promise I would never have an abortion. "I promise, Grandma", I said, a bit bewildered. No matter I was only 12 years old and didn't quite like boys yet. This sweet lady watched the church bulletins for the funeral announcements. Grandma attended countless funerals of people she was not familiar with only because she thought they deserved a big send off. My other grandma scolded the telephone operator one day. The operator asked if she would accept a collect call from me to which Grandma replied, "Of course I will—this is my granddaughter calling!" This grandma was the best cook in the region. On short notice Grandma could take meager fare and put together a feast. Both ladies supported me in all endeavors and taught me so much about respect, generosity, and unconditional love. Ministering angels with aprons on.

There is an aunt who is more than family—she is a friend and kindred spirit. We have shared many things like movies and painting ceramics. She taught me to crochet, to love tacos, and play canasta. I taught her to drive a car. She drove me all over, whether it was to Bible study or for a hot fudge sundae. My favorite times together are in study and discussion of God's Word. We taught Bible class together to a wide range of children, and even took it on the road to the local children's home. Auntie put legs to my imagination. Health and circumstance have caused us both to cut back from a lot of the old activities, but she is still one of my biggest encouragers and confidents. A ministering angel.

God brought two special Irish angels into my life some ten-plus years ago. They came to us as God called our beloved dad Home. They helped us through those hard days. But, their more important role was to lead us to a deeper relationship with God. These two opened up the Holy Word for me personally, and showed me how to apply the truths to my life. They taught me how to take my shovel and dig for the jewels within the Word—all the while not missing those lying on the surface. They truly showed me that the Bible was a "Book of Instruction Before Leaving Earth". And now, even from so many miles away, they still work as my mentors, my friends. Ministering angels—with an accent.

In December, 2007, I suffered a major heart attack along with respiratory arrest. It was a critical time for our family. They all gathered around at the hospital within a short notice of this event, each bringing his or her own means of support. While I was hanging by a fine thread between life and death, my family nearly fractured from such a heavy load. Then came Chaplin Amy. She brought sandwiches and coffee to sustain the family during those long hours of waiting. Because of her unique role in the hospital, Chaplin Amy was able to slip in/out of the area where doctors worked franticly to keep me alive. She would whisper a prayer in my ear even though I was unaware of her presence. Then Chaplin Amy would return to my family and pray with them. The day after I regained consciousness, Chaplin Amy came to me in the critical care unit. She came close and whispered, "We are so thankful to have you back. What can I do to make you more comfortable?". Granting my request,

Chaplin Amy leaned close, bending over the bed rail and granted my requests. Twinkling blue eyes set in an angelic face, surrounded by auburn curls, Chaplin Amy sang a favorite hymn of her grandma's, and then prayed with me. A blessed ministering angel.

Age is not a factor to angels. Mom, at age 83, continues to minister to me day in, day out, taking care of all my needs. My baby niece, at age 18 months, ministers to me with her sweet smile and infectious giggle. And all of them in between continue to uplift me and encourage me in their own special ways. No one on earth has ever felt so loved and cared for as I am. My fervent prayer is that I can in some small way minister to them, to help them grow in their own relationship with God. And, when the time comes that I must leave this band of earthly angels, I will be met by God's Heavenly beings and escorted to be with the Source of ministering angels. May you be blessed with your own ministering angels. And may we always remember—"*Be not forgetful to entertain strangers: for thereby some have entertained angels unawares.*" (Hebrews 13:2)

...they that wait upon the LORD shall renew their strength; they shall mount up with wings as eagles; they shall run, and not be weary; and they shall walk, and not faint.
~ Isaiah 40:31 ~

THANK YOU TO ~

~ Thank you to my family for inspiring me and encouraging me to put my thoughts down on paper....

~ Thank you to Eddie and Margaret McGuiggan for putting my thoughts straight, and pointing me to our Lord....

~ Thank you to all those people who saw me for something more than a crooked woman...

~ Thank you to those who may read this booklet —may you be touched in a good way and grow spiritually from something written on these pages....

Printed in the United States
207573BV00001B/204/P

9 781606 477298